CONTENTS

PRINCIPAL BOOKS CONSULTED

The United States: The Presidents, the Parties, and the Constitution by Herbert Agar (Eyre and Spottiswoode, 1950)

Memoirs by Prince von Bülow (Putnam, 1931)

Twenty-Five Years by Viscount Grey (Hodder and Stoughton, 1928)

King Edward VII by Sir Philip Magnus (Murray, 1964)

The Ottoman Empire and Its Successors by W. Miller (Cambridge University Press, 1936)

King George V: His Life and Reign by Sir Harold Nicolson (Constable, 1952)

The Evolution of American Foreign Policy by Dexter Perkins (Oxford University Press, 1948)

Au Service de la France by Raymond Poincaré (Paris, Librairie Plon, 1926)

La Question d'Extrême-Orient, 1840–1940 by P. Renouvin (Paris, Hachette, 1947)

MAPS

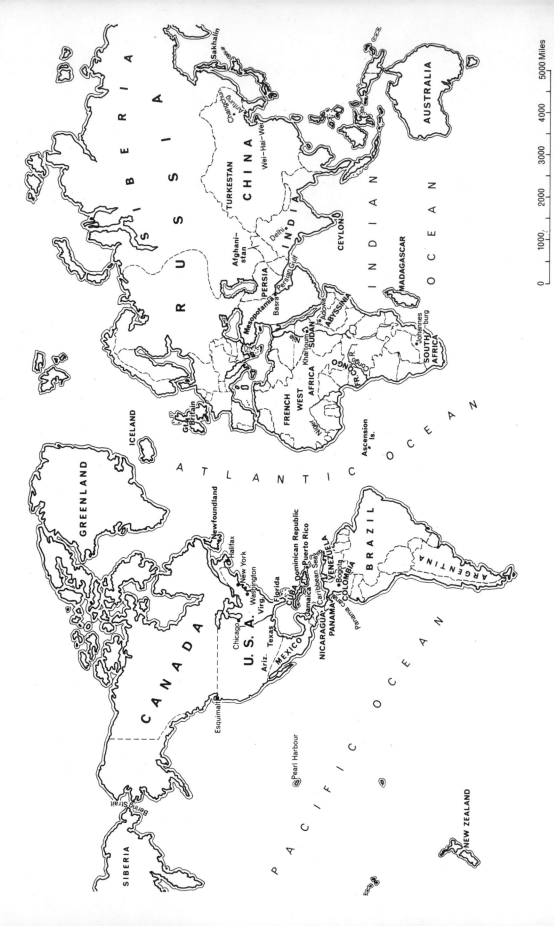

MAP NO. I THE WORLD AT THE TURN OF THE CENTURY

1 The World at the Turn of the Century

THE WORLD at the beginning of the twentieth century was a very different place from what is was to be two generations later. Primarily this was so because Europe was still the centre of the universe, both politically and economically, and Europe was still in the main the Europe of the *ancien régime*. Great Britain was the foremost maritime Power with no continental commitments, just as Germany was the greatest land Power. The United States was still a debtor country, and neither the United States, Italy, nor Japan claimed the status of World Powers. Spain was temporarily in eclipse. The partition of Africa between the Great Powers was still in uneasy, if spectacular, progress. The British Commonwealth of Nations had not yet replaced the British Empire, but there was still a United Kingdom of Great Britain and Ireland, over which 'Queen Victoria, by the Grace of God of the United Kingdom of Great Britain and Ireland, Defender of the Faith, Empress of India', bore sway. Four great empires, Germany, Austria-Hungary, Russia, and Turkey, dominated continental Europe east of the Rhine, just as three great empires, the British, the Russian, and the Chinese, dominated Asia. It was a glittering façade, but it was little more. The appearance of a European order was preserved by the immense forces of tradition and sentiment, as well as by the fear universally felt by elder statesmen of all countries that even the most modest attempts at repair or readjustment would bring the whole structure to ruin.

As Europe was the only continent that really mattered, so its groupings were the only ones that carried any real weight, and they were, on the one hand, the Triple Alliance of Germany, Austria-Hungary, and Italy, and on the other the Dual Alliance of France and Russia. Great Britain played a much less prominent part in the politics of the mainland of Europe in the latter years of the nineteenth century than had been the case in its predecessor or was to be the case in its successor, and there were several reasons for this, of which two are outstanding. The accession of Queen Victoria in 1837 severed the link with Hanover which had existed ever since George I came to the throne in 1714, and so obviated the necessity of intervention in Germany whenever a crisis arose there. Then, again, domestic and – later – Imperial politics tended to absorb the attention of successive British administrations, not to mention that of the British public, so that in the main there was a gradual withdrawal from Europe save when the national interests were vitally affected.

This state of affairs was, however, already beginning to be modified somewhat, and the situation was well summed up by Sir Edward Grey, then Foreign Secretary, in a statement to the Committee of Imperial Defence in the spring of 1911, when he said,

> I must go back rather an alarming way to the time when I first became Under-Secretary at the Foreign Office in 1892. . . . The situation then, and for some years previously, had been this: that the two restless Powers in Europe were France and Russia. . . . The solid quiet group . . . was the Triple Alliance of Germany, Austria and Italy. It had been the policy of Lord Salisbury before 1892, and it was the policy of Mr. Gladstone's

1   Sir Edward Grey (1862–1933; *left*), the British Foreign
Secretary, on his way to the House of Commons. He played
a leading part in negotiations aimed at keeping the peace
in Europe.

Government of 1892, not to join the Triple Alliance or come under definite commitment to it, but generally in diplomacy to side with the Triple Alliance as being the
stable Power in Europe, and the one which was securing the peace. . . . Soon after 1892
the situation began slowly to change.

There were several reasons for this quite apart from the dismissal in Germany in
1890 of the old Imperial Chancellor, Prince Bismarck, by the young Kaiser Wilhelm II;
indeed, even if he had remained in office it is by no means certain that circumstances
would have allowed him to pursue his old policy. To avoid difficulties with Great
Britain he had abstained from the creation of such a navy as the position of Germany
in the world might seem to warrant, and he had refrained from direct interference in
the Near East for fear of driving Russia into the arms of France which happened after
his fall from power. Nevertheless, the German Empire had become a commercial and
colonial Power of the first rank, and as such could hardly be expected to leave her
shipping unprotected; while there were evident signs of a Near Eastern crisis in which
German traders and gunboats might rival British ones.

To some extent, of course, the impetuosity of the new German Emperor contri-
buted to the breach with Bismarckian traditions in foreign affairs; he was rash and
tactless, and he did not realise the full implication of much that he said and did: nor
did he know when to stop, though that, it must be admitted, is a knowledge with
which singularly few monarchs and statesmen have been endowed. At the same time
Wilhelm II was throughout his life the sport, rather than the master, of circumstances,
and if he was restless during the opening years of the twentieth century his subjects
were becoming restless too. The generation which had been content to rest on its laurels
after three victorious wars was passing away, and its successor was bent on winning

8

2   German militarism. The Kaiser takes the salute at a march-past of his Grenadier Guards on the Unter den Linden in Berlin.

triumphs of its own. Moreover, Bismarck had Prussianised the whole Reich, with the result that the German people were becoming imbued with that aggressive spirit which had hitherto characterised only the Prussians; in a way, indeed, it is even true to say that Bismarck had himself rendered impossible the continuance of his own policy.

All this, however, does not necessarily mean that the changes to which Sir Edward Grey referred rendered the outbreak of the First World War inevitable; on the contrary, there were many occasions between 1900 and 1914 when a different decision might have averted it, but that this was not the case was largely due to the absence of a single controlling hand in Berlin and to the growing aggressiveness of the German people. While Bismarck was at the helm the foreign policy of the German Empire was directed by a single brain and will. Thereafter German policy was never again controlled by a single hand, and in the years to come it represented an unstable compromise between the views of the Kaiser, the Imperial Chancellor for the time being, and the Foreign Office.

When the new century began Great Britain was involved in a war in South Africa against the Dutch republics of the Transvaal and the Orange Free State. It had begun in October 1899 and was theoretically caused by the refusal of the *Volksraad* in the Transvaal, of which State Paul Kruger was President, to give political rights to immigrants of Anglo-Saxon origin, but there was a great deal more to it than that, and it was in fact a struggle between the Dutch and the British for supremacy in South Africa. In these circumstances it is not surprising that the conflict should be viewed from different points of view. Save on the part of a small minority it was considered in Great Britain that it was a just war because the Boer republics had denied to British citizens their lawful rights, but European public opinion saw only the moral right of the Boers to do what they liked in their own country, and regarded the struggle as a further example of the British fondness for browbeating small nations. 'In this war I am on the side of England', the Austrian Emperor, Franz Josef, observed to the British Ambassador at a diplomatic reception, but his attitude was exceptional. Elsewhere throughout the world Britain was regarded as a bully, and scorned as an incompetent one at that.

Incompetence there certainly was, and upon an extended scale. The British government had convinced itself that the Boers would yield to pressure without fighting, and so had paid little attention to the advice of its military advisers: what preparations it did make were at once tardy and inadequate. Both sides under-valued alike the resources and the resolution of its antagonist. The Boers, who had the most vivid recollection of an earlier struggle with Great Britain from which they had emerged victorious, who knew the extent of their own armaments, and who were well aware of the insignificant number of British troops in South Africa before the outbreak of hostilities, believed that the government in London would prove to have neither the means nor the will to wear down their determined resistance, and that in any case it would not be long before some European Power came to their aid.

On the British side there was also complete ignorance in high places as to the nature of the warfare which was about to take place. Regular troops are always at a disadvantage in dealing with a mobile force of irregulars on its own ground, and the farmers of the Dutch republics were irregulars of quite exceptional quality. Born and bred on the African veldt they were familiar from boyhood with the rifle, the saddle, and the transport-wagon; they possessed, too, the obstinate patience of their race, and on their hardy ponies they could move at a speed – before the days of the internal combustion engine – which baffled the British generals. Nor was this all, for they had the good fortune to produce some remarkable leaders such as Christian de Wet, a Free State farmer; J. H. Delarey, a Transvaaler, who distinguished himself as a skilful commander of mounted infantry; and, above all, Louis Botha, who displayed both strategical and tactical ability of the highest order. Indeed, had it not been for the lax discipline of the Boers, their inability to act on a large combined plan, and their excessive caution, the war might have lasted a great deal longer than was actually the case.

In the small battles fought during the opening months of the campaign it became

3   The Boer War. General Louis Botha (1862–1919; *extreme left*) discusses tactics with his officers.

4 President Paul Kruger of the Transvaal Republic ('Oom Paul'; 1825–1904) with his wife. During the Boer War he left South Africa to seek refuge in Holland.

apparent that, due to the use of smokeless powder, the old fear of a visible foe had been replaced by the paralysing sensation of advancing on an invisible one. A universal terror, rather than a localised danger, now enveloped the attacker, while the defender, who was always ready to protect himself by some rough earth- or stonework, was enabled because of the rapidity of rifle fire to use extensions unheard of in former wars, and in consequence to overlap every frontal infantry attack. Thus at the Battle of the Modder River the Boers extended 3,000 men on a frontage of 7,700 yards; at Magersfontein 5,000 on 11,000; and at Colenso 4,500 on 13,000; yet in spite of this human thinness these fronts could not be penetrated.

After Cronje's surrender at Paardeberg to Lord Roberts on 18 February 1900, the Boers took to guerrilla warfare, when the war proper may be said to have begun, and by the time it finished on 31 May 1902 it had absorbed in all 450,000 British soldiers, many of whom were mounted infantry. It was brought to a conclusion by an audacious scheme which struck at the Boer mobility, for a vast network of fenced blockhouse lines was woven over thousands of square miles of the theatre of war, which was split into a number of areas, and these were one after another cleared by mounted columns. It was a long process of attrition, but it was an eminently successful one. The South African War may be summed up in the statement that it cost Great Britain two and a half years of hard fighting, and the expenditure of a hundred and fifty million pounds, before a population numbering little more than fifty thousand adult males was finally reduced to subjection.

The war shattered the complacency which had been so prominent a characteristic of Victorian Britain, and which had reached its height at the time of the Queen's Diamond Jubilee in 1897. That pageant was over, and Britain's lath-and-plaster reputation had been tested by fire and steel. At home the results were in the long run salutary, for although the administration after 1902, a Conservative one with A. J. Balfour at its head, did little or nothing to apply the lessons of the war, the advent of the Liberals to power in 1905 brought to the War Office the greatest Secretary of State for War that Great Britain has ever known, namely R. B. Haldane. His view was that the security of the British Isles demanded not only the possession of a powerful navy, but the provision of appropriate land forces as well, and he realised that, in addition to meeting this first call upon its resources, the country ought to be capable of undertaking certain operations abroad. For this purpose the regular troops serving in the United Kingdom, together with the army reserve, were made to form the Expeditionary Force, while the Militia was converted into a Special Reserve charged with the duty of training and providing drafts for the regular units at the front. These constituted what was known as the first line, and the second line, composed of the Yeomanry and the old Volunteers, became the Territorial Force of fourteen infantry divisions and fourteen mounted brigades for Home Defence.

Outside Britain the results of the South African War were distinctly damaging to British prestige. The difficulty which her army experienced in overcoming the resistance of the Boers caused it to be rated extremely low by the General Staffs of the continental

5   The guard of Boer miners at Kimberley. The town held out under siege for 126 days from October 1899 until February 1900. The inhabitants, loyal to the British, had two armoured trains, a feature of the war on the British side, and even succeeded in making one or two excursions in them.

Powers, and this depreciation continued until the First World War. In these circumstances it is hardly remarkable that the rally of the self-governing Dominions to the cause of the Mother Country, and the evidence of Imperial solidarity which this afforded, should have escaped the notice of foreign Powers, prophetic though it was of future developments. Indeed, it was only Britain's absolute mastery of the sea that prevented her European rivals from coming to the aid of the Boers.

Such being the case there were three courses open to the British government. The first was to maintain its naval strength and continue the policy which had come to be known as that of 'splendid isolation'. If that were neither practicable nor desirable it might be well to seek an understanding with Germany, with whom Britain had been on friendly terms for many years, even if relations had been none too cordial of late. In the third resort, France might be approached, though that would mean burying a hatchet which had been flourished both in London and Paris for many a long year. Each of these policies had its distinguished protagonist. The leading advocate of the first was the Marquess of Salisbury, Prime Minister from 1895 until the end of the South African War; of the second, Joseph Chamberlain; and of the third, when the second failed, Joseph Chamberlain, and, later, the Marquess of Lansdowne.

In a static world isolation was unquestionably the best policy, but even the Prime Minister was beginning to doubt how much longer the world was likely to remain static, and isolation had recently proved to be the reverse of 'splendid'. By the end of the war there was no question but that Britain was isolated, and informed opinion was in consequence becoming very frightened: to continue it was clearly dangerous, so there was really no choice in the matter – recourse must be had to an ally of some sort on the mainland of Europe.

The obvious choice was Germany. Her monarch was Queen Victoria's grandson; there was an immense amount of goodwill towards her in Britain which had not been seriously dissipated by recent unfriendly acts on the part of her government; and memories of the way in which the Prussians had come up in the nick of time to save

6 Robert Gascoyne-Cecil, Marquess of Salisbury (1830–1903), Prime Minister 1895–1902. His policy was to keep Britain out of European alliances.

Wellington at Waterloo were still rife. There were many advantages to Britain in having Germany on her side, and an agreement with her had much to recommend it. She was a potential challenge to British naval supremacy, and she was already competing actively with Britain for the world's export trade. She was militarily the most formidable Power in the world, she had a rising population, and a long tradition of forceful and forward diplomacy. Clearly she could become incomparably Britain's most dangerous enemy, and a settlement with her was therefore the more desirable. Nor was this all, for as a friend she was in a good position to put pressure on Russia, as she had done in Bismarck's time, and Russia, before her defeat by Japan, was a serious rival to Britain in the Middle and Far East.

13

Even before the old century came to an end negotiations had begun, but it soon became clear that the German government was waiting on the progress of events in South Africa, and the Imperial Chancellor, von Bülow, spurned Chamberlain's advances. When, however, the Boer armies were in flight, and the General Election of 1900 had returned the Salisbury administration with a relatively unimpaired majority, Chamberlain set to work again. He told Baron von Eckardstein, with whom he was dealing, that the moment had come for Great Britain to abandon her policy of isolation, and to link herself either with Germany or with France and Russia. He said that he would himself prefer closer relations with Germany, and in his opinion a beginning could best be made by a secret agreement concerning Morocco, where German interests were continually growing in importance: they were chiefly represented by the Mannersmann brothers who were soon to press their government to declare a protectorate over the Sus region, where they were acquiring land containing ore deposits. If the German government refused, Great Britain would be obliged to make a treaty with Russia, even at the price of considerable sacrifices in China and on the Persian Gulf.

Accordingly negotiations were resumed in January 1901 and they dragged on for some six months, but, warned by his previous experience, Chamberlain left the principal part in the conduct of them to the Foreign Secretary, Lord Lansdowne. The man who did most to frustrate them was one of the officials in the German Foreign Ministry, a Baron von Holstein, for he kept instilling into the Kaiser and Bülow the belief that Great Britain had always pursued the policy of getting others to pick her chestnuts out of the fire, and that this was why she wanted an agreement with Germany. He doubted the possibility of an understanding between London and Paris, and held that therefore Germany was in a position to sell her friendship at a very high price. Meanwhile, Chamberlain was becoming increasingly restive, though Bülow remained deaf to warnings that the British statesman's attitude was changing, while in the summer

7   Bernhard Prince von Bülow (1849–1929) was Chancellor of Germany from 1900 to 1909 and firmly resisted all suggestions of an Anglo-German alliance.

The Times openly advocated an understanding with Russia, and called attention to the growing strength of the German navy. As the months passed an Anglo-German alliance was seen to be a mere dream, and the following winter witnessed an exchange of polemics between Chamberlain and Bülow which marked the end of the attempt to arrive at an understanding between Berlin and London. In the circumstances it is difficult to resist the conclusion that Great Britain would have become the ally of Germany, and the First World War would not have taken place, had it not been for the misguided attitude of the Kaiser, the Imperial Chancellor, and, above all, Baron von Holstein.

A friend of some sort on the mainland of Europe, however, Britain must have. As at the time of the War of American Independence she was discovering the disadvantages of isolation, and that she could not exert her proper influence in the world unless she had an understanding with a continental Power. It is true that she had not, during the South African War, been in so great peril as in the War of American Independence, but that was partly because the European States were more divided in 1900 than in 1780, and partly because Lord Salisbury had paid far more attention to the navy than did Lord North. All the same, the universal hostility to Britain which was evoked by the campaign against the Boers was a warning which no British government could afford to neglect.

Isolation and an agreement with Germany having proved impossible recourse was had to an understanding with France – not that there was much about contemporary conditions in that country to endear it to a Britain just emerging from the Victorian era. First of all she was the only substantial republic in Europe, and the Britain of those days was essentially aristocratic. She was traditionally England's enemy, and a mere thirty odd years before she had been allowed to go down before Germany with only a polite murmur of sympathy from London; furthermore, the two nations had recently been on the verge of war over Fashoda – an incident which, although it took place just before the end of the nineteenth century, must be described if the bad feelings which marked the contemporary relations between Great Britain and France are to be fully appreciated.

Fashoda, which has since been renamed Kodok, is in the Sudan, on the west bank of the Upper Nile, some 460 miles south by river of Khartoum. In July 1898 Major Marchand arrived there from French Equatorial Africa, and hoisted the French flag. Two months later Kitchener conquered the Sudan from the Dervishes at the decisive Battle of Omdurman outside Khartoum, and advanced south to find the tricolour flying over Fashoda. It was clear that a crisis of the first magnitude had arisen.

The French force consisted of 8 French officers or non-commissioned officers and 120 black soldiers drawn from the Niger district. Sir Winston Churchill, in *The River War*, wrote a graphic account of the meeting between the British and the French:

> The Sirdar [i.e. Kitchener] and his officers . . . were thrilled with admiration at the wonderful achievements of this small band of heroic men. Two years had passed since they left the Atlantic coast. For four months they had been absolutely lost from human ken. They had fought with savages; they had struggled with fever; they had climbed mountains and pierced the most gloomy forests. Five days and five nights they had stood up to their necks in swamp and water. A fifth of their number had perished; yet at last they had carried out their mission.

15

Kitchener and Marchand met on terms of the most perfect courtesy, and when the English General disembarked the Frenchman came out to meet him with a guard of honour. The two men shook hands warmly. 'I congratulate you,' said Kitchener, 'on all you have accomplished.' 'No,' replied Marchand, pointing to his troops, 'it is not I, but these soldiers who have done it.' Kitchener, telling the story afterwards, remarked, 'Then I knew he was a gentleman.' All the same Marchand refused to withdraw his force unless he received instructions from Paris to that effect, and the French government declined to give way.

Public opinion on both sides of the Channel was soon inflamed. Sir Michael Hicks-Beach, then Chancellor of the Exchequer, bluntly declared, 'There are worse evils than war, and we shall not shrink from anything that may come.' The Liberal leader, Lord Rosebery, assured the government that behind it was 'the united strength of the nation', and he continued, 'If the nations of the world are under the impression that the ancient spirit of Great Britain is dead, or that her resources are weakened, or her population less determined than ever it was to maintain the rights and honour of its flag, they make a mistake which can only end in a disastrous conflagration.' The Press, too, was for the most part decidedly bellicose, and a cartoon in *Punch* well represented the popular attitude. 'What will you give me if I go away?' asks the little organ-grinder. 'I will give you something if you don't,' replies a muscular John Bull with a menacing frown. The Reserves were called up, and naval preparations were made.

Public feeling ran just as high in France, where it was chiefly directed against Joseph Chamberlain, then Colonial Secretary, who was believed to be the villain of the piece. *Liberté* referred to him as a 'renegade Radical, sexagenarian dandy . . . who has once again put in the pocket of his correct frock-coat the powerful and corpulent Marquess of Salisbury'.

In the event of hostilities Britain's strategic position was very strong. Aerial warfare was a development far in the future, and another eleven years were to elapse before the first aeroplane flew the Channel. The British navy was infinitely more powerful than any other in the world, and the submarine was as yet in its infancy. The French army was undoubtedly much stronger than anything Britain could put into the field, but as an invasion of England was out of the question (and the English were not likely to make any attempt to invade France) it would not be of much use, while in a naval war France stood to lose her overseas possessions. Even on the narrower issue of Fashoda itself Britain was in the right, for the place was indisputably in the Sudan, the rest of which Kitchener had reconquered from the Dervishes.

All the same Salisbury had to go carefully, a fact which was not always apparent to his more hot-headed colleagues, and to that section of the Press and public which was clamouring for extreme measures. A war between England and France would be used by Germany as a means of blackmailing both parties, while although Russia had no desire to be implicated she might come to the aid of her ally if the latter was too hard-pressed. She was in any case on the worst of terms with Great Britain, and would be only too delighted to give her a rap over the knuckles if the opportunity arose.

While the issue thus hung in the balance, far away in Addis Ababa, the capital of Abyssinia, the British Minister, Rennell Rodd, was taking action which was to weigh the scales in favour of peace. It was known that reinforcements were on their way to join Marchand, and that they would be crossing Abyssinian territory. The Foreign

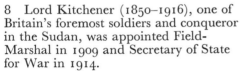

8   Lord Kitchener (1850–1916), one of Britain's foremost soldiers and conqueror in the Sudan, was appointed Field-Marshal in 1909 and Secretary of State for War in 1914.

9   Fashoda, 1898. While waiting for Kitchener to arrive, Col. Lord Edward Cecil (*centre*), Lord Salisbury's son, introduces Captain Keppel to Major Marchand (*left*).

Office therefore told Rodd that it was of the utmost importance that this force should be stopped, but that the international situation was so delicate that he must in no circumstances encourage the use of force.

So Rodd went to see Menelik II, the Emperor of Abyssinia, who was always a good friend of England, and asked him to take steps to see that the Frenchmen were not provided with either guides or bearers. Menelik said that he could not do this as he had given his word that they should have both. Nothing would persuade him to go back on his promise, and Rodd returned to his Legation a very sorry man. Next morning, however, the Emperor sent for him, and said, 'It is true that I gave my word that the French should have guides and bearers, but I did not promise that these should remain with them.' So after the expedition had set off for two or three days the guides and bearers were withdrawn; the column was immobilised; and Marchand was not reinforced.

For six weeks the French government hesitated, then the news arrived in Paris that the reinforcements would not reach Fashoda, and Salisbury's firm, but unprovocative, diplomacy bore fruit; Russia definitely declared that in the event of war France would have to fight alone. In these circumstances there was nothing for it but to order Marchand to withdraw, and in March 1899 an Anglo-French Convention was signed by which the watershed between the Congo and the Nile became the boundaries between the two countries.

The ease with which a settlement was ultimately reached cannot obscure the danger that was averted. Had Salisbury displayed any sign of weakness Russia would have come to the aid of France in the hope of settling old scores with England; in that case Britain would have been thrown into the arms of Germany, for whose support she would have had to pay a very high price. On the other hand, had he adopted the bellicose tone desired by some of his colleagues war with France would have been inevitable, and the British and French would have sunk each other's ships – a state of affairs that could only have been of benefit to Germany, especially as she was now beginning to build a fleet of her own.

Internally, too, the Third French Republic appeared to be deficient in soundness, stability, and repute, for a succession of weak ministries, the violence of faction, and a series of financial scandals had led France more than once to the verge of civil war. Above all, there was the *Affaire Dreyfus*, which was far from being concluded, and which was splitting the country from top to bottom.

Its origins lay in the fact that in the closing years of the nineteenth century there was within France an outbreak of spy-mania. The country was recovering from the disaster of 1870, and under the inspiration of Freycinet a military instrument had been created capable of confronting Germany; such being the case it was only natural that the German government should feel some concern, and should try to discover the plans of the French General Staff, together with the secrets of its armaments. Long before the Dreyfus case broke espionage had begun to develop: two traitors had already been discovered and condemned, of whom one was a clerk in the Ministry of Marine and the other an officer in the technical branch of the artillery. The intelligence branch of the War Office was thus already on the alert, and it had no doubt that the German military attaché, Schwartzkoppen, was directing an espionage system in conjunction with his Italian colleague, Panizzardi.

The central document in the charges against Dreyfus was what was known as a

10 In January 1899, during an impassioned debate on the Dreyfus Case in the French Chamber of Deputies, the Socialist leader Jaurès was attacked by the conservative deputy de Bernis.

18

bordereau, and around this the battle raged for twelve years. It was, indeed, an explosive document, not only in itself but because it was the fruit of a theft committed in the German Embassy in Paris, and the abstraction of documents from the inviolable residence of a diplomatic representative was quite enough in itself to create a serious incident. For that reason Hanotaux, the Foreign Minister, was of the opinion that a prosecution should not be launched, but he was overruled.

Suspicion was not immediately attached to anyone. It was clear that the sender of the *bordereau* took part in the life of the General Staff, and must be an artillery officer. The list of documents given to Schwartzkoppen also led to inquiries among the officers undergoing Staff instructional work, and who of necessity passed through the successive bureaux of the Staff. A process of elimination and the resemblances of handwriting led finally to the charge being made against Captain Alfred Dreyfus. He was condemned by a court martial without being found in the act of guilt, and without confessions being recorded either by the prosecution or by the tribunal. The defence had accordingly pleaded not guilty. The explanations tantamount to confession which handed Dreyfus over to military degradation were subsequently contested.

At an early stage after this it was stated that Dreyfus had been found guilty after the communication of secret documents, and because he was a Jew. His judges were suspected of being influenced by an anti-Semitic journal. From then until his rehabilitation in 1906 the rights and wrongs of Dreyfus divided France.

To the average Englishman at the turn of the century it seemed but the climax to a long catalogue of sordid events which revealed a nation deeply divided and with a governmental system which neither received nor deserved the loyal support of the people. Above all, the fact that it was in France in 1899 that the first Socialist entered a European Cabinet, in the person of Alexandre Millerand, much later to be deposed from the Presidency for being too far to the Right, was not likely in those days to be reassuring to a Conservative administration in Whitehall.

In spite of these and other obstacles a settlement was in due course reached on all the points at issue between Great Britain and France, and in this connection mention must be made of the work of King Edward VII himself. It would be untrue to say that he initiated, or even played the leading part in, the negotiations which took place, but it is extremely doubtful whether they would have been successful without him. He created the atmosphere in which the statesmen of the two nations were able to collaborate, and the turning-point was his visit to Paris in May 1903. In the days of his youth he had been a great favourite, but since then a great deal of water had flowed under the bridges. Such being the case this visit to Paris was one of the most critical episodes of the King's life, and as he drove down the Champs-Élysées, on his way from the Bois de Boulogne Station, the crowd was sullenly respectful, and only a few hats were raised; here and there, too, were to be heard cries of 'Vivent les Boers', 'Vive Marchand', and 'Vive Fashoda'. 'The French don't like us', somebody remarked to the King. 'Why should they?' came the royal answer, and the King set to work to make them change their opinions.

He neglected no opportunity of impressing upon his hosts his desire to be their friend, and one incident will serve to illustrate the scrupulous attention which he paid to detail. One evening, accompanied by his suite, he went to the Théâtre-Français. The house was indeed full, but the audience was icy, so during the interval the King left his

19

box to see what could be done to win this hostile crowd to his side. In the lobby he saw a French actress whom he had met in London, so, holding out his hand, he said, 'Oh, Mademoiselle, I remember how I applauded you in London. You personified there all the grace, all the *ésprit* of France.' Never had he better displayed his almost uncanny ability to say and do the right thing; for, as may be supposed, the remark spread like wildfire, and the ice was broken. The incident, moreover, was typical, for in the streets and at official receptions, in public and in private, the King exerted all his tremendous powers of charm, with the result that when he left Paris the route was lined with a madly enthusiastic crowd, so that where there had been cries of 'Vivent les Boers' there were now loud shouts of 'Vive notre Roi'. This visit should surely be classed among the greatest personal triumphs in the history of the British Royal Family. It is little wonder that years later Poincaré should have said of the King, 'Not one of my fellow country-men has forgotten the happy impetus given on that decisive occasion by His Majesty King Edward VII to the work of concord which has outlived him.'

The protagonists in the negotiations which ensued were Lansdowne and Delcassé, and the result, in April 1904, was a series of agreements which collectively initiated what was known as the Anglo-French Entente. As this was to prove the most important diplomatic event in the early years of the twentieth century, and as it was to survive until the fall of France in the Second World War, it is necessary to examine its clauses rather closely.

The first of these concerned Egypt and Morocco. Great Britain declared that she had no intention of altering the political status of Egypt, then a semi-independent Turkish province of which she was in occupation, and France undertook not to obstruct British action there by asking that a limit of time be fixed for the occupation, or in any other way. France, in her turn, declared that she had no intention of altering the political status of Morocco, where she was in much the same position as was Britain in Egypt, and Britain promised not to obstruct French action in that country. Both in Egypt and Morocco there was to be commercial liberty for at least thirty years, and no fortifications were to be erected on the Moorish coast opposite Gibraltar. For the rest, France was to come to an understanding with Spain concerning Morocco; the Egyptian government was given a free hand in financial matters so long as the interest on the debt was paid; and the legal position of the Suez Canal in time of war was settled in accordance with the wishes of France.

A second agreement removed a long-standing difference relating to the fishing rights off Newfoundland. France now renounced these rights, and in return Great Britain agreed to certain territorial modifications in West Africa, in consequence of which France obtained 14,000 square miles and uninterrupted access from her possessions on the Niger to those on Lake Chad.

Yet a third document contained a declaration concerning Siam (now Thailand), Madagascar, and the New Hebrides. The two Powers agreed to refrain from armed intervention, or the acquisition of special privileges, in the basin of the Menam; France recognised that all Siamese possessions on the west of this neutral zone and of the Gulf of Siam, including the Malay Peninsula and the adjacent islands, should come under British influence; and Britain admitted French influence in all Siamese territory on the east and south-east of the zone. As regards Madagascar the British government abandoned the protest which had been maintained since 1896 against the tariff introduced

11   2 May 1903, the climax of King Edward VII's State
visit to Paris. The King salutes the French regimental flags
during the great military review at Vincennes.

after the annexation of the island by the French. A special arrangement, it was decided, was necessary in the case of the New Hebrides, and in 1906 an Anglo-French condominium was duly established there.

Such was the inception of the Anglo-French Entente which was to play such a prominent part in diplomacy during the years that lay ahead. It was far from being an alliance, and it did not profess to do more than settle the problems which had long been outstanding between the two Powers, but it prepared the way for a closer understanding when circumstances arose, and only a short time was to elapse before this happened. In retrospect it can be seen as a step in the direction of war for it did much to crystallise the division of Europe into two armed camps, for there was no longer any doubt where Great Britain stood. Yet on the face of it nothing seemed happier or more reasonable than this mutual liquidation of vexatious colonial grievances, and the House of Commons was delighted with an arrangement which secured the position of Britain in Egypt, but Lord Rosebery, the Liberal ex-Premier, who noted that Germany, the strongest military Power in Europe, had not been consulted over Morocco, was critical, saying in private that the *Entente Cordiale* with France would eventually lead Britain into a German war.

Not the least important of the repercussions of the Anglo-French Entente was its effect upon the relations between Russia and Britain, though it was some years before this was fully felt. The two countries had been on the worst of terms during the greater part of the nineteenth century, and they had come within an ace of war as recently as 1877–78. Since then the policy of Russia had undergone a modification, for her

21

experiences in Bulgaria, where those whom she had liberated from the Turks had proved singularly ungrateful, in the eighties had disgusted her with the affairs of South-East Europe, and her rulers' attention was increasingly attracted by the Far East, where the dying empire of China seemed to offer greater prizes. In these circumstances they wanted to feel that they could be sure of support in the West, and thus there had come into existence that Dual Alliance of Russia and France to which allusion has already been made.

Even before the fall of Bismarck relations between Paris and St Petersburg had become a little closer, though it was not easy for Alexander III to overcome his objections to a republican France. In 1888 there had been negotiated the first French loan to Russia, and in succeeding years it was followed by further financial transactions which strengthened the ties between the two countries. In 1890 the Russian government placed an order for rifles in France, and gave an assurance that they would never fire upon Frenchmen. Nor was popular support lacking in either country for this new policy. 'L'empire des Tsars est à la mode', wrote a Belgian diplomatist from Paris as early as 1888, and two years later a fellow countryman reported that 'the infatuation for Russia has gained all classes', while 'the contrast between the institutions of the two countries is not felt in Paris'. In Russia it was the same, and when a French squadron

22

visited Cronstadt in 1891 the sailors were astonished at the enthusiasm with which they were received. The climax was reached when, after the French naval band had rendered the Russian national anthem, the Tsar ordered a Russian band to play the 'Marseillaise', hitherto forbidden in public places, and he himself heard it standing and uncovered.

With the ground thus prepared, it became possible to go a little further, and before the end of that same year, 1891, a political agreement was reached between the two Powers, who declared that in future they would confer on every question of a nature to threaten the maintenance of peace, while if this were in actual danger, and especially if one of the two countries was menaced by aggression, the two governments agreed to concert measures. This was not yet an alliance, but one was clearly foreshadowed.

Two more years elapsed before the final step was taken in Paris and St Petersburg, and the military convention of December 1893 was concluded. Briefly, this provided in various ways for the contingency of an attack by the Triple Alliance. If France were to be assailed by Germany, or by Italy with German support, then Russia was to attack Germany: similarly, in the event of an onslaught by Germany on Russia, or by Austria-Hungary with German backing, then France was to come to the aid of Russia. Various clauses defined the means by which the two Powers were to co-operate, and stipulated that they would not conclude a separate peace. That an alliance had been concluded was generally known, but it was not officially announced until the beginning of 1895, and in the following year the new Tsar, Nicholas II, visited Paris where he received an ovation.

The German government was, with good reason, profoundly disturbed at the course which events had taken, and Wilhelm II did everything in his power to point out to the Tsar the dangers of the policy his Ministers had adopted, while Bismarck in his retirement angrily complained that by their attitude towards Russia his successors in office had cut the telegraph wire to St Petersburg. In the London of those days the Franco-Russian Alliance met with equal disapproval as might have been supposed in the light of Sir Edward Grey's appreciation of the situation at that time; it was felt that both parties to it would become more aggressive, and trouble was in consequence apprehended in regard to questions arising out of the situation in Alsace-Lorraine and the Near East. For France the conclusion of the alliance was a notable triumph; it meant that she had recovered sufficiently from the disaster of 1870 to be regarded as a desirable ally, and that her period of isolation was at an end. Russia, indeed, cared less about prestige than her new ally, but she had expensive ambitions in the Far East, for which she hoped the French investor would pay. Actually, both Powers were a good deal weaker than appeared on the surface, as the events of the next ten years were to prove, and it was not until the weight of the British Empire was thrown into the scale that the new group was a match for its older rival. The brilliance of French diplomacy at this time, largely due to the skill of the Cambons in London and Berlin and of Barrère in Rome, barely concealed the weakness of French arms or the putrefaction of French politics. Russia had feet of clay as the Japanese were shortly to prove, while her political system was already undermined.

Of the only other European Powers of importance the Dual Monarchy of Austria-Hungary was firmly integrated in the Triple Alliance. As in the case of Russia her internal condition left much to be desired, though for entirely different reasons; as a multiracial State she suffered from all the disadvantages attendant upon the rising tide

23

of nationalism. On the throne was the Emperor Franz Josef, who had been there since 1848. Posterity has rightly been kinder to him than were his contemporaries. It was not in his nature to court publicity in the manner of Wilhelm II, and after the disasters of his earlier years he played no great part upon the European stage, but in his own dominions he attempted to put into practice that doctrine of the balance which he had learnt from Metternich, who had presided over the destinies of Austria from 1815 to 1848, in his youth. He had displayed uncommon shrewdness in the sixties when he had met the demands of Hungary, and had he adopted the same line with the Czechs it is at least doubtful if their autonomist movement would have assumed an anti-dynastic form. However, it would be unfair to blame him unduly, for it was the same mistake that Queen Victoria made with regard to Ireland, and King Alfonso XIII in respect of Catalonia. Had Queen Victoria paid a quarter of the attention to Ireland that she paid to Scotland, some, at any rate, of the troubles of the last hundred years might have been avoided: as it was, during her whole reign she spent less than five weeks in Ireland, while her visits to Scotland covered nearly seven years.

The Emperor proved to the very end of his life that he had not forgotten the teaching of Metternich to avoid extremes, and one of his last acts was to refuse to agree to the establishment of a military dictatorship in Bohemia. Circumstances, however, were against him, and as the years passed his German allies and his Hungarian subjects joined hands to upset the balance upon which the régime depended. Berlin regarded the Austro-Hungarian Empire merely as a subject State whose duty it was to supply troops to take Russian pressure off the Reich, and when necessary to die for the greater glory of the Prussian King. The Slavs were the enemies of Germany, so Vienna must outlaw them too, irrespective of the fact that the Habsburgs had always numbered millions of Slavs among their most loyal subjects. This policy suited the Magyars, whose own treatment of minorities left a great deal to be desired, so that what can only be

13 King Alfonso XIII of Spain (1886–1941). The warmth of his reception in Catalonia, where separatism was rife, in 1908 caused him and his government to re-establish constitutional guarantees. But tension and violence soon returned.

14 King Victor Emmanuel III (1869–1947; with binoculars and white trousers; *front*) pays a visit to the battleship *Regina Elena*. The Italian fleet was to play an important part in Italy's designs on North Africa and the Mediterranean.

described as an unholy alliance was made between Prussia and Hungary, and this went far to undermine the very foundations upon which the Habsburg monarchy rested. Franz Josef resisted this tendency with all his ebbing strength, but unfortunately owing to age his powers of resistance were at their weakest when they were most required, that is to say in the summer of 1914.

The third member of the Triple Alliance, namely Italy, was in an even more equivocal position, for Austria was her hereditary enemy, and she had only agreed to bury the hatchet – temporarily, as events were to prove – because of her antagonism to France. It was not so much that certain European territories of France, such as Savoy, Nice, and Corsica, tempted Italian cupidity, as that French policy in Africa was disturbing the minds of Italian statesmen. They were very sensitive – not without reason – about their country's position in the political equilibrium of the Mediterranean, and this seemed to be endangered by the extension of French power along the northern coast of Africa. At the same time when Italy joined the Triple Alliance her representatives made it clear that they had no hostile designs where Great Britain was concerned, and to the treaty was attached a Declaration by Italy, confirmed by Germany and Austria-Hungary, to the effect that the alliance could not 'in any case be regarded as being directed against England'. Italy's Mediterranean interests clashed with those of France, not with those of Great Britain.

Finally, sprawled across the Balkans, the Near East, and part of North Africa, was the Ottoman Empire – 'the Sick Man of Europe' to use a phrase coined by the Tsar Nicholas I. Sick the Turk might be, but he was an unconscionable time in dying, and

25

his potential legatees were becoming more than a little restive. The delay in his demise was due to two main factors, namely his fighting qualities, and the skill of his ruler, Sultan Abdul Hamid II. In the last years of the nineteenth century an Armenian revolt had been crushed, and the Greeks decisively beaten; while as for the Sultan himself, with all his faults, which were many, he had proved, and was proving, capable of holding his ramshackle dominions, composed of men of many different races and creeds, together, which when their time came proved to be beyond the capacity of his successors.

It must not, however, be supposed that at the turn of the century the Great Powers never acted together, for there was a grouping of Austria-Hungary, France, Germany, Great Britain, and Russia, with Italy tagging along a little behind, known as the Concert of Europe, though it must be admitted that its members often played out of tune: still it was due to the Concert that the wars between the lesser States did not develop into a general conflagration, as might otherwise have so easily been the case. It was only when, in the summer of 1914, the questions at issue vitally affected the Great Powers themselves at first hand that the Concert proved unable to take any effective action to preserve the peace.

MAP NO. 2   NORTHERN AND EASTERN EUROPE

2 Great Britain at Home and Overseas

GREAT BRITAIN in 1900 was an aristocratic community, and this fact was reflected in the attitude of both the Conservative and Liberal Parties which divided the political stage between them. There was, in effect, a governing class divided into two parties, and for this there had not yet been substituted two party machines each with its own class basis, which was to be one of the more significant developments of the years that lay ahead. Unfortunately, this governing class reproduced all the worst characteristics of high French society before the Revolution, for it tried to have the best of both worlds, in that it drew all the practical advantages which came from settled habit and custom, such as extreme reverence for private property, but at the same time it could feel 'advanced', being firm in the conviction that the challenges to all conventional morality could be trusted to remain inside the covers of the appropriate books. It was a governing class which too easily spared itself effort. Most of its members were content to be morally and intellectually passengers, and many of them disloyal passengers at that.

The Victorian Age, which was just coming to an end, has been much misrepresented, with the result that Victorianism has become rather a dirty word, and to call anybody or anything Victorian is almost a term of abuse, suggesting that they or it are thoroughly out of date. Yet it was an age of great beginnings, and most of the things in life which are now taken for granted had their origin at that time. From whatever standpoint it is regarded it was certainly not static.

At the apex of the British political system stood the monarchy, which was in an infinitely stronger position than had been the case only a few decades earlier, when there had been a definite republican movement. That this should have been the case was largely due to Queen Victoria, who was now in the last months of her long life. She early realised that if a monarch is to be the effective representative of a nation he or she must in a civilised community be personally the object of respect. With all his faults her grandfather, George III, understood this, and in consequence always retained his hold upon the affection of his subjects. The character of George IV was such that loyalty to him personally was an impossibility for the mass of the people, and though William IV was somewhat more estimable in his private life, his whole outlook was that of a retired ship's captain. The throne had lost its dignity, and there was a reversion to the days of the first two Georges. Had Queen Victoria resembled her uncles the monarchy would have been most unlikely to have survived.

On 22 January 1901 she died. 'A fiery English patriot', the late H. A. L. Fisher wrote, 'and in English politics a fierce partisan, she retained to the end, despite shattering toil and responsibility, the sentimental heart of a German girl.' One of her Prime Ministers admirably summed her up when he said that if he wanted to know the reactions of the middle class he always asked the Queen's opinion. Queen Victoria was succeeded by her eldest son, Albert Edward, who took the title of King Edward VII. He was fifty-nine when he ascended the throne, and it may well have been that it would have been better had he done so at an earlier age. In domestic politics he was not particularly interested, and he had the reputation of being a Liberal in his views: where foreign affairs were concerned it was very different, and he played no inconsiderable personal part in them, as we have seen.

The Conservatives had been in power, under the Premiership of Lord Salisbury, since 1895, but there was a General Election in 1900. As it took place during the South African War it became known as the 'Khaki Election', and it was marked by considerable bitterness, for the opponents of the government maintained that Ministers were taking an unworthy advantage of the patriotic feelings roused by the war, and they particularly resented the slogan, 'A vote for the Liberals is a vote for the Boers.' The result of the election, however, was to leave the Parliamentary situation practically unchanged, for the Conservatives had a net loss of a mere nine seats, which left their voting strength in the House of Commons to all intents and purposes unimpaired, so the Ministry was entitled to claim that it had received a vote of confidence in its policy. The conclusion of the South African War was marked in British domestic politics by the replacement of Salisbury as Prime Minister by his nephew, A. J. Balfour.

It would be difficult to exaggerate the change which gradually came over British public life in the years which followed the turn of the century. The carefree days which had immediately preceded it were never to return, and the year 1900 was the last occasion on which the Income Tax was to stand at eightpence. The war in South Africa had itself revived much of the bitterness in political circles which had been dying down since the days of the Home Rule Bills, while a year after peace was signed with the Boers the commencement of the campaign for Tariff Reform added fresh fuel to the fire. From then until 1914 there was a savagery in British politics, in and out of Parliament, for which it is necessary to go back to the closing years of the reign of Queen Anne to find a parallel: how far all this affected the ordinary man-in-the-street is another matter.

The first cloud on the horizon was the introduction of an Education Bill in the autumn of 1902. Into the details of that measure it is unnecessary to enter, but the principle it laid down was that of rate aid for Church and other voluntary schools. In those days the antagonism between the Church of England and the Nonconformist bodies was infinitely greater than it has since become, and the memory of the fierce disputes over educational matters in the previous generation was sufficiently vivid to add fresh fuel to the flames kindled by the new Bill. 'Rome on the rates' became a popular cry. How, it was argued, was it just that a Baptist should pay rates for the support of a school pervaded by an Anglican or Roman atmosphere? Still more acute was the complaint that in single-school areas, of which there were some eight thousand up and down the country, Nonconformists were compelled to send their children to Church schools. The debate, which raged furiously in all quarters, brought out all the latent jealousy of Romanism, Anglicanism, and the alleged domination of the squires in the rural areas, and it lost the Conservatives the Nonconformist vote which had largely been theirs since the split in the Liberal Party over Home Rule in the mid-eighties. So strong was the feeling that by the end of 1903 more than seven thousand summonses had been issued against people who 'passively resisted' payment of the Education Rate in England, and distraint sales of their goods had taken place in over three hundred cases: in the following year these figures were trebled.

Temperance was another question which much concerned Liberal opinion. The evil of drunkenness was very real in those days, and it was generally acknowledged to

15 The General Election of January 1906. Supporters of
Mr Arthur du Cros, the Unionist candidate, are taken by
motor-waggon to the polls at Hastings.

be such, while its connection with crime and social misery was regarded as established.
Many remedies were proposed, such as total abstinence, local option, and the curtail-
ment of the number of public houses. In these circumstances it was considered as a
distinctly retrograde step when an Act was passed in 1904 which treated the publican's
licence as a property from which he could not be dispossessed without compensation
(save in the case of abuse) by the licensing justices. To the opposition which was
gathering against the Balfour administration on the score of its education policy there
was now added the indignation of all the temperance workers in the country.

All this, however, was nothing compared with the criticism caused by the proposal
to introduce indentured Chinese labour into the South African mines. The British Trade
Unions, which had by now built up for themselves a position of authority unequalled
by any similar organisation in Europe, saw in this scheme a menace to the standard of
life which had only been reached by the persevering effort of three generations. All the
old bitterness between Capital and Labour was revived in full force, for if cheap labour
could be transported from China to Johannesburg why, it was asked, should not the
capitalists fill the mills of Lancashire and Yorkshire with inexpensive and submissive
Orientals? If that were done it required no great stretch of imagination to guess what
would become of the British working-man, for wages would fall and the standards of
life would decline. In actual fact, of course, the chances of Oriental labour being introduced into the British Isles were exceedingly remote, but the fear of it was for a time
very real, and there can be little doubt but that 'Chinese Slavery' was an important
ingredient in the wave of feeling which in 1906 swept the Liberals into power.

Above all, there was Joseph Chamberlain's campaign for Tariff Reform, which he
launched in 1903, and which was to divide the country for many a long year. To
understand the bitter feelings which were roused it must be remembered that the

29

system of Free Trade had governed Britain for sixty years, during which time it had experienced an astonishing expansion of national prosperity, and the fact that the zenith had already been passed was not generally noticed. In particular, shipping and shipbuilding, banking and coal-mining, profited by freedom, and could only be injured, it was considered, by the imposition of tariffs on foreign manufactured articles and the same reasoning applied to London as the monetary centre of the world. At the same time it was true that other countries, notably Germany and the United States, had notably prospered under Protection; but against this it was argued that British goods still went all over the world, so that despite high duties abroad the old Free Trade maxim that foreign markets could be conquered by cheapness still seemed to make sense.

As against this Chamberlain unfurled the picture of a great Empire bound together by fiscal ties. The home country was asked to place protective duties on imports, including food and raw materials, primarily in order that it might give the colonies a preference against the foreigner, but also as a shield against foreign competition at home. What neutralised Chamberlain's appeal was the fact that there did not appear to be any need for a change, and also that the 'hungry forties' in the days of Protection were still a living memory, easily revived at the least mention of a tax upon food. The first result of this campaign was to split the Conservative Party from top to bottom, and the second to pave the way for an overwhelming Liberal victory at the polls. The Conservative Party which in 1900 had a majority of some 130 now found itself in 1906 in Opposition with only 157 seats in all.

The new Prime Minister, Sir Henry Campbell-Bannerman, possessed none of the shining qualities which had marked the five previous holders of the office, but he was an admirable chairman, and he knew exactly how to make his very difficult team work, which was well, because he was in fact presiding over the most brilliant administration that Britain had known since that of Lord Liverpool at the beginning of the previous century. Several of his colleagues, indeed, took the view that he was not really capable of leading the House of Commons, and that one of their number would do it much better, therefore it would be as well for him to go to the Lords: the Prime Minister did not share their apprehensions, and he resisted all efforts to persuade him to leave.

The General Election of 1906 was the first sign that the old order was coming to an end. Among the handful of contemporaries who realised the fact was Sir Wilfrid Laurier, then Prime Minister of Canada, and he wrote to Professor Hewins in London, 'The recent elections have undoubtedly opened a new era in the history of England. The England of the past may survive partially yet for a few years, but it is a democratic England which now takes its place. The Labour element will count henceforth as a very important factor, and it is difficult to foresee exactly to what extent, but certainly to a very large extent, it will control legislation.' If this statement was in some respects to prove an exaggeration, subsequent events have shown that there was much truth in it, and although the turning-points in the lives of nations are not so clearly defined as some authorities would have us believe, it is difficult to resist the conclusion that the year 1906 represents a very definite landmark in the annals of Great Britain. It was then that the nineteenth century really ended, though its ghost was to walk until 1914; social and economic rather than political problems became the more important: while abroad the *status quo* which had existed relatively intact for nearly two generations, was beginning to give evidence of its approaching collapse. The writing was on the wall.

During these years both the Liberal and Conservative Parties were to some extent untrue to their traditions, while loudly proclaiming their devotion to them. The Liberals, driven to the Left by the loss of the Whigs in 1886, increasingly sponsored Socialistic measures which would have horrified their former leaders, though fate had willed it that this policy should ultimately benefit not them, but the rising Labour Party. The Conservatives, on the other hand, seemed to have lost the impetus which they had received twenty years before by the accession of Joseph Chamberlain and his Liberal Unionists, and also to have forgotten what Disraeli had taught them in the matter of social reform. In actual fact the General Election of 1906 was to be the last great Liberal triumph, and it was at this time, in its hour of victory, that the Liberal Party began to show signs of disruption and weakness. As it became more markedly democratic the City of London and the financial interests which had previously supported it tended to find a new political home with the now urbanised and commercial Conservatives. Furthermore, the predominantly middle-class support which the Liberals received was one cause of their failure to recognise the rising economic claims of the workers, with the result that many Radicals were turning in the direction of Labour.

At the same time it cannot be denied that the Liberal government of 1906 effected a great deal. It gave South Africa self-government, and it pleased the Trade Unions by emancipating them from the liabilities imposed by the Taff Vale decision. Old Age Pensions were allowed out of State funds for the first time, Workmen's Compensation was extended, National Health Insurance and Unemployment Insurance were introduced, and Trade Boards were set up to fix minimum wages in sweated industries. The more ambitious measures, such as the Licensing and Education Bills, were rejected by the House of Lords, and this in due course precipitated a constitutional crisis of the first magnitude, which was the more acute since the views were diametrically opposed.

16 At a meeting in Birmingham in 1904 Joseph
Chamberlain (1838–1914) asks his audience if they can tell
the difference between a Protectionist loaf and a Free Trade
loaf.

17   James Keir Hardie (1856–1915), the pioneer Labour leader, speaks at a meeting in Trafalgar Square, London. Behind him is Mrs Emmeline Pankhurst, the suffragette leader.

To the government and its supporters it seemed intolerable that under a Constitution which was nominally democratic, a party, however numerous its majority, and however fresh its mandate from the constituencies, should have its legislation indefinitely blocked by a hereditary Second Chamber, and they declared that such a veto was an indefensible anomaly. The Conservatives, on the other hand, believed that any weakening of the powers of the House of Lords would open the floodgates to the tides of revolution which they saw surging through the world, and in particular would pave the way for Home Rule for Ireland, to which they were specially opposed. Both sides, it may be added, were equally sincere in their attitudes.

The storm broke in all its fury in 1909, when the Lords took the unprecedented step of rejecting the Budget which had been introduced by David Lloyd George, who had become Chancellor of the Exchequer in the previous year when Asquith succeeded Campbell-Bannerman as Prime Minister. Its main provision was the taxation of the increment on land values, but there was also a super-tax on incomes of over £5,000 a year; death, legacy, and succession duties were raised; and the liquor trade was placed under heavy contribution. In defending his proposals Lloyd George set the tone for the campaign which was to follow when he said that it was a war Budget for waging implacable warfare against poverty, and thereafter it was generally known to those who approved of it as the 'People's Budget'. It was introduced in the House of Commons in April, but it was not passed until 5 November, so violent was the opposition which it provoked: on the 30th of the same month the Lords, by 350 votes to 75, passed a resolution to the effect that 'This House is not justified in giving its consent to this Bill until it has been submitted to the judgement of the country.' The challenge was at once accepted by the government, and a General Election took place in January 1910. So far as they could the Liberals fought on the demerits of the Lords, and the Conservatives on the merits of Tariff Reform, which proved to be their trump – if only – card.

As soon as the final results from the whole country were available it was at once obvious that an extremely difficult situation had arisen. The great Liberal majority of 1906 had disappeared, and in the new House of Commons the strength of the Parties was: Conservatives 242, Liberal Unionists 31, Liberals 275, Labour 40, and Irish Nationalists 81. The government losses, it may be added, were almost entirely confined to England, where the Conservatives and Liberal Unionists even had a slight majority over all their opponents. The interest taken by the electors in the issues at stake is emphasised by the fact that no less than 92 per cent of them went to the poll. The question immediately arose – Had the government received a mandate from the country to force the Budget through the House of Lords? The Liberals maintained that such was clearly the case since the Conservatives were in a minority in the new House; but to this it was objected that the Irish were opposed to the Budget, and that if they voted according to their convictions Ministers would be in a minority.

To pass to the appearance of Labour upon the political scene, which took place during the opening years of the twentieth century, and where its activities were in due course to be as revolutionary as those of the internal combustion engine. The British Labour Party did not take its present name until 1906, when it first appeared as a substantial party in the House of Commons, having won thirty seats. It had been founded six years earlier, as the Labour Representation Committee, and it was the direct descendant of Keir Hardie's Independent Labour Party which had come into existence in 1893. The I.L.P., out of which the Labour Party grew, was the immediate outcome of the spread of the New Unionism, ushered in by the great London strikes of gas-workers and dockers in 1889. The New Unionism brought large numbers of less-skilled workers into the Trade Union movement, and led to big changes in Trade Union policy; while the Reform Acts of 1884 and 1885 were also favourable to the growth of the working-class movement because they had extended the franchise to the less-skilled. These workers, and the new leaders who represented them, wanted improved conditions

18 Sidney Webb (1859–1947), with his wife Beatrice a prominent member of the Fabian Society, was an indefatigable writer on Socialist themes and later became a Minister in the first Labour government.

33

19 A comfortably off upper middle-class family group in
Edwardian England.

and greater security: the slogans of the New Unionists and of the I.L.P. were the legal
eight-hour day, the legal minimum wage, and the Right to Work. The I.L.P. further
gave its allegiance to Socialism, which had previously been represented in Great Britain
by the Marxist Social Democratic Federation, but the new Socialism for which it stood
was evolutionary and undogmatic, and its immediate concern was social reform. Its
leaders were much influenced by the Fabian Society: *Fabian Essays* had been published
under Bernard Shaw's editorship as long ago as 1889, and Sidney and Beatrice Webb
were engaged in producing tracts about the distribution of wealth.

     Under Keir Hardie's guidance the I.L.P. set out to persuade the Trade Unions to
support independent working-class political action, but this was by no means the
innovation that might be supposed, for the miners had been acting in this way ever
since the Reform Act of 1867 had given the vote to a section of the workers in the towns.
What was new was that whereas in the past the Trade Unionists who were returned to
the House of Commons had attached themselves to the Liberals, they were now urged
to cease this practice: seven years of intensive propaganda partly achieved its purpose,
and the Labour Representation Committee was born.

     At first its growth was slow, but the Taff Vale Judgment of 1901, which in effect
made strikes almost impossible by threatening the Unions with actions for damages
caused by them to employers, brought many more Unions in, and greatly increased the
political keenness of all. Somewhat paradoxically Labour joined with the Liberals in
opposition to Tariff Reform, and it won nearly all its thirty seats in 1906 with Liberal
support. It was able to secure the passage of the Trade Dispute Act of 1906, and it
succeeded in putting on the Statute Book the first Act authorising the feeding of children
at school. On the other hand, it received a severe blow by the Osborne Judgment of

20 Domestic servants at Henley Regatta, always a notable
event of the London season.

1909, which declared all political action by Trade Unions to be unlawful, and thus knocked away the financial foundations of the Labour Party. In these circumstances it was forced on the defensive in the two General Elections of 1910, so all it was able to do was to defend the seats it already held, and to contest a very few others. It just about held its own, and its apparently increased strength was due to the fact that the Miners' Federation, whose representatives in the House of Commons had sat as Liberals up to 1909, had joined it in that year.

It is in no way surprising that these developments should have taken place, for if Edwardian England represented the acme of comfort and well-being for the well-to-do and a large part of the middle class, such was far from being the case where the mass of the population was concerned. It is true that the condition of the worker, especially in the towns, was infinitely better than it had been a couple of generations earlier, but the depressed classes had come to realise that they were depressed, and in increasing numbers they were determined that they would not be depressed any longer. Among the poorest classes, where the income was below the 'living wage', there was practically no margin left when the demand for food was satisfied. 'For the incomes below thirty shillings, two-thirds of the total income is spent on food,' a Board of Trade investigator has left on record, 'while in the case of incomes of forty shillings and above, about fifty-seven per cent is spent on food.' Of the total expenditure on food one-fifth went on bread and flour, while tea, in the lowest income groups, called for ninepence farthing a week and sugar for eightpence. Housing conditions, though slowly improving, still left a very great deal to be desired. In these circumstances it is no wonder that Lloyd George should have rallied the proletariat to him when he said at Limehouse, 'It is a hard thing that the poor man should have to fight his way to the tomb through the

35

brambles and thorns of poverty. I am going to cut a new path for him, a longer and an easier one, through fields of waving corn.'

Yet it would be a gross exaggeration to suggest that the working classes were wholly deprived of the amenities of life, particularly in the matter of entertainment and sport. The music-hall flourished until 1914; the cinema was everywhere making its appearance; and football and cricket attracted large crowds. Soccer was particularly popular in the North of England, and it is interesting to note that between 1900 and 1914 not a single southern club achieved the headship of the First Division of the Football League, though in the F.A. Cup during the same period the balance was to some extent redressed by the Spurs, Aston Villa, and the Wolves. The shape of coming events was seen in 1905 when Middlesbrough paid Sunderland a transfer fee of £1,000 for A. Common, the first player to command so high a figure. As for cricket, it was the Golden Age, with Grace still playing in first-class matches, and Hobbs, Jessop, and C. B. Fry in their prime. Racing, too, was another popular sport, and when King Edward VII won the Derby with Minoru in 1909 the enthusiasm throughout the country was immense among all classes, not least among the workers.

At the other end of the social scale the opening years of the twentieth century specially favoured the *rentier* and the successful professional and business man; a moderate fortune could be accumulated without undue effort, and Income Tax stood at little more than a shilling in the pound. Travel was cheap and easy, and house rents were on a reasonable scale. Nor was this all, for overseas investments were between two and three thousand million pounds, and they brought into Great Britain an unearned increment of several hundred million sterling a year. The country lived on its overseas trade and these investments, but to understand the situation existing in the fourteen years before the First World War it is necessary to forget that of today.

London was still in the main the London of the Victorian era; it was very definitely the capital of an empire upon which the sun never set; and the central scene of a now

21 Working-class poverty in the East End of London.

22 Miss Marie Lloyd (1870–1922), star of the English Music Hall. She was a specialist in cockney comedy and introduced such songs as *Oh Mr Porter*.

vanished age. At the beginning of King Edward's reign motor cars were rarely seen, hansom cabs and open or closed carriages being the recognised means of transport.

Ladies riding in Rotten Row used side-saddles, though their habits no longer came below their ankles, and they were usually followed by a mounted groom. Numbers of people rode there every morning between nine o'clock and one, while in the summer, particularly after church on Sunday, under the trees along the Ladies' Mile or on the grass opposite Stanhope Gate, much of London fashion was to be met. There were tan riding-tracks along Constitution Hill and Birdcage Walk, by which a few Members of Parliament still rode down to Westminster, and as late as the First World War at least one judge arrived at the Law Courts on horseback each morning. Unmarried girls in society seldom walked out without a maid, and they were always taken to dances by chaperones. Ladies wore long skirts brushing the ground, tightly laced corsets, and, in the evening, eighteen-button gloves reaching to their armpits, and they carried fans. Top-hats and frock-coats, particularly when the Court was in residence, were the ordinary dress of gentlemen of leisure, of whom there were plenty on from four to five hundred pounds a year, who spent much of their time shooting, hunting, and fishing on their richer friends' estates, or lunching and dining with them in London.

The great mansions such as Devonshire, Lansdowne, Montagu, Grosvenor, Dorchester, Stafford and Spencer Houses, all now destroyed or turned into clubs or public offices, were inhabited by their owners. It is true that there were a few million-aires from the United States and South Africa, but although there was plenty of comfort and some luxury, there was surprisingly little ostentation compared with more recent times. The majority of people probably lived within their incomes, even if they did not save as much as in Victorian times, for in spite of the South African War and Sir William Harcourt's Death Duties, the Income Tax, as we have seen, remained round

37

23 Knightsbridge, London, in 1908. The last horse-bus of the London General Omnibus Company ran in October 1911. Though the first motor-buses had appeared in London between 1898 and 1903, the successful B type motor-bus was not introduced until October 1910.

about the moderate figure of from 6*d*. to 1*s*. in the pound, while super- or surtax was unknown. A house in St James's Place could be rented for £200 a year, and a staff to run it – cook, parlour-maid, and house-maid – cost £64. In effect, for very many people life was a pleasant and easy round, and even the small *rentier* could live comfortably.

King Edward VII had been on the throne for some years before there was any general relaxation of the customs which had obtained during the later decades of his mother's reign, and when change came it began in the highest ranks of society – the customs of the middle classes were hardly affected when the First World War broke out. Social relationships were subject to a rigid code of etiquette. All women who had any social pretensions had 'At Home' days to which they strictly adhered. When a man paid a call he took his hat, stick, and gloves into the drawing-room, for to do otherwise was to lay himself open to the charge of behaving as if he were at an hotel. Attendance at a dinner or a dance necessitated a formal call soon afterwards.

Edwardian travel was still very much an upper- and upper-middle-class affair: for the mass of the population holidays with pay were a matter of the future. An exception was domestic servants, who received a fortnight's holiday with salary, but after that they were entitled to board wages if their employer did not require their immediate services. It was, incidentally, generally estimated that the keep of a horse and a domestic servant was about the same. In these circumstances Bank Holidays really meant something: absenteeism, in the modern sense, was rare for there was a good deal of unemployment (it was not until 1912 that unemployment benefits came into being), and an employee who took time off would soon find himself out of work, which meant that he and his family would starve, a state of affairs which was also likely to be the sequel of a strike.

It was during these years that the Press as we know it today came into existence, and this development will always be associated with the name of Alfred Harmsworth, better known as Lord Northcliffe. On 4 May 1896 there appeared the first number of the *Daily Mail* – the Popular Press had been born, and journalism was never to be the same again. Northcliffe's policy was to give the public what it wanted, or what he induced it to think it wanted, and to present the news in such a way that it could be taken in at a glance. The *Daily Mail* cost a halfpenny, so there was no class of reader who could not afford it, but in 1907 Northcliffe spread his wings more widely and acquired *The Times*. The political influence of the Press, however, was of relatively slow growth, and it is to be noted that at the General Election of 1906, although most of the newspapers in the country were supporting the Conservative Party, it suffered the greatest defeat in its history: apparently Northcliffe could persuade his readers to grow sweet peas, but not to vote for Tariff Reform.

It is difficult to resist the conclusion that although the power of the Press was building up during the early years of the present century it did not reach its apogee until the First World War. By that time Northcliffe had become possessed of an influence such as no newspaper proprietor has ever exercised before or since, for with *The Times* and the *Daily Mail* both under his control he could spread his views with equal effect among the classes and the masses, and in his heyday he was responsible for half the circulation of the London Press. It must also be remembered that the newspapers of those days had virtually no competition to face: the power of the pulpit and the platform, which had been considerable in Victorian times, was rapidly waning, and wireless as a means of disseminating news, had not come into existence. There were also quite a large number of newspapers from which to choose, both in London and in the big provincial cities, while most significant where the future was concerned was the appearance of the illustrated daily, and by the end of the period the *Daily Graphic*, the *Daily Mirror*, and the *Daily Sketch* were already in existence. The London evening papers, it may be added, had a very small circulation, and at the height of its influence the *Westminster Gazette* never had a circulation of more than 20,000.

The Edwardian Press naturally reflected Edwardian social habits, and that accounts for the pre-eminence of the serious weeklies at that time. They were originally published on a Saturday morning, and were read over the week-end by those who had either received them by post (there were Sunday deliveries of letters in those days) or

24   Alfred Harmsworth, Lord Northcliffe, (1865-1922; *right*), pioneer of the popular Press and owner of *The Times*. With him is Sir Cecil Spring-Rice, a distinguished British ambassador to the United States (*see p. 86*).

39

had bought them on their way home from their offices on Saturday afternoon. The Sunday newspaper was unknown in any respectable household, and in an age when the Victorian sabbath was still observed there was plenty of time to peruse a weekly from cover to cover before Monday morning. In these circumstances it is little wonder that men like Lord Robert Cecil, later third Marquess of Salisbury and Prime Minister, thought it an honour to contribute to the *Saturday Review*.

London, however, was not England, as Paris was France, and the great provincial cities played a very important part in the national life; indeed, many of the religious, political, and social movements had their origin outside the capital. In 1909 it was estimated that nine out of ten families in the larger centres of population had migrated there from the countryside within three generations, but those who had settled in London found very different conditions from those who had made their homes in the provinces. The Londoner's house rent was immeasurably higher, for the mean weekly price of two rooms in the capital was six shillings, while elsewhere it was little more than half that amount; for four rooms the variation was between nine shillings in the one and five shillings in the other. The working-class flat was in the main a thing of the future, although it was much in evidence on the Continent: but the English had not yet taken to it, and were still struggling to maintain in the urban aggregation to which they had migrated some semblance of a home. This desire explains the enormous acreage of chimney-pots and tumbled cottages which was revealed in what has been termed 'a kind of smoky grandeur' which met the eyes of the Edwardian visitor as he was borne along the railway embankments of South and East London.

The passage of time has caused many misconceptions to arise with regard to the social conditions of the past, and no illusion is more persistent than that in the provinces the Sunday of sixty years ago was a day of gloom and misery. In reality, nothing could be further from the truth, though it was very different from what it has since become. Games were not usually played either in public or in private; those who had their own carriages would never have dreamed of taking them out on a Sunday; and church-going was universal except, perhaps, with the very lowest class of the community. At the turn of the century a Russian visitor, Alexandre Benois, the great balletomane, wrote that 'life stands still in England on Sundays'. In effect, Sunday was a day of rest, and as such it met a definite need, for if the businessman of those days did not work any harder than now he worked longer hours: the head of a firm was at his office by nine, and he rarely left it until five-thirty, while he never took Saturday morning off as a habit. There was no compulsory early closing, the shops did not shut before eight, and the mass of the population worked a full six-day week, so a rest on Sunday by no means came amiss.

Nor was this all, for getting about was by no means easy before the coming of the motor-car. North Wales, now the playground of South Lancashire, is a case in point, for, save for a few places like Llandudno, it was very remote. Within a few years a change came over the scene, and what had necessitated a week-end's holiday became accessible in a few hours' run on a Sunday afternoon. All this led to an inevitable relaxation of established habits, and the outbreak of the First World War found both metropolitan and provincial society with a very different outlook from that which had characterised it at the death of Queen Victoria.

If the great provincial cities and the small provincial towns were more than holding their own when King Edward VII succeeded his mother the same was not, in the main,

25 Two old peasant villagers in Devonshire. During the Edwardian period the young and active were leaving the villages to seek work in the towns, and the population of certain country areas became predominantly one of old men and women, and children.

the case with the countryside: it presented a sorry spectacle, for apart from certain favoured neighbourhoods, and the specialised population which served the needs of the country-houses, it was hastening to decay. No one stayed there who could possibly find employment elsewhere, and all the young people with energy and initiative forsook the life of the villages and fields for that of the towns. The peasantry was unique in Europe in its complete divorce from the land, and it found no attraction in the cheerless toil of an agricultural labourer upon what was a scanty wage. The villages increasingly tended to be left, while the ancient skilled occupations were becoming lost arts.

There were several reasons for the miserable state of the countryside, and at the beginning of the twentieth century the immediate cause was the agricultural slump in the seventies. The mechanical inventions, and particularly the improvement in the means of communication and transport, gave powerful assistance to the process which had been going on since the end of the eighteenth century, and led to a further transfer of population from the villages to the towns, so that by 1901 no less than 77 per cent of the inhabitants of the United Kingdom were resident in urban districts. While the towns and their suburbs showed a rapid increase at each decennial census, the purely agricultural areas, including the whole of Ireland except the north-eastern corner, were almost stationary or actually retrogressive. The opening up of new countries beyond the seas, and the development of oceanic and railway transport, combined to bring into England those supplies of cheap foreign food and raw materials which were as valuable to the manufacturers as they were detrimental to the agricultural interest. The acreage

41

under wheat and other grain crops declined steadily, and, as we have seen, the labourers left the land to seek employment in the mills and factories. National prosperity, as measured by manufacturing production and the statistics of imports and exports, was at its highest level in 1873, when Great Britain was called upon to make good the destruction of capital caused by the Franco-German War; but in the years that followed a succession of bad harvests told heavily on agriculture, and prices were further depressed by the extension of wheat-growing in the United States, which was now pouring grain into England.

There was no permanent recovery in the rural economy after this. In 1874 the area under wheat in the United Kingdom was in the neighbourhood of four million acres, but by the Queen's death it had fallen by considerably more than half; other arable crops also declined, though not to the same extent. At the same time the average freight per quarter of wheat by ship from New York to Liverpool fell from 5s. 6d. in 1871 to 10d. in 1901, so that the imports of wheat per head of the population doubled, and those of meat quadrupled, between 1870 and the end of the nineteenth century. In effect, although the general wealth and productive activity continued to grow, the agricultural interest had no share in this expansion, and it is to be noted that the value of land, as assessed for Income Tax, was eleven millions lower in 1899 than it had been thirty years earlier. The average agricultural wage in 1901 was 1s. 8d. per day.

For two generations, that is to say during the Victorian period, the desolation of the countryside was materially aided by the supersession of the road by the railway. For many years after the coming of the 'iron horse' the highways sank into a deep somnolence, from which it appeared that they would never reawaken, and in some places they even became grass-grown from little use; in due course the bicycle made its appearance, and that brought a little life back to them, but places without a railway-station were

26   A house party at Kilkenny Castle, Ireland. King Edward and Queen Alexandra (*left*) are seated on the sofa with the Marchioness of Ormonde. Princess Victoria, the King's daughter, is seated on the extreme left.

still very cut off from the outside world in the early years of King Edward VII. The Edwardian period witnessed the rapid development of the motor-car and consequently the rebirth of the road: this was in no small measure due to the example of the King.

It could be argued that the impact of the internal combustion engine on the English way of life was even more far-reaching than that of Marxism. The King's first trip in a motor-car took place two years before his accession when Mr Scott-Montagu, M.P., drove him in a 12-h.p. Daimler at Highcliffe while he was staying there with friends. In those days motoring was regarded as a very low affair, and quite unworthy of royal patronage, but by March 1902 the King was the possessor of several cars, and he had made a long motor-tour in France. Considerable pressure was put on him to use a 'motor-coach' at his Coronation, and he was by no means unwilling to assist the nascent British motor industry in this way, but when it was pointed out to him that such a vehicle would have to be without noticeable vibration, noise, vapour, or smell the King reluctantly decided that the proposal was unworkable.

All the same, he continued to be a great patron of motoring, and garages were constructed at Windsor, Sandringham, and Buckingham Palace: his own first choice of cars was a Daimler and a Mercedes, and he understood something about their engines. In 1905 King Edward became the Patron of the Automobile Exhibition at the Crystal Palace, and two years later of its successor at Olympia; while in 1907 he added the title of Royal to the Automobile Club, and in 1909 – with rare prescience – to the Aero Club. His cars were always known by the fact that they alone in the kingdom bore no number-plate. It may be noted that this proclivity did not meet with his mother's approval, and Queen Victoria was not attracted by a photograph of her eldest son in an open motor, wearing a tall hat which had been shaken or blown over his nose. 'I hope', she told the Master of the Horse, 'you will never allow any of those horrible machines to be used in my stables. I am told that they smell exceedingly nasty, and are very shaky and disagreeable conveyances altogether.'

Even as late as 1909 the journey from Oxford to Shaftesbury took a single day, and it was not always easy to get petrol. One motorist in Somerset in these early times on asking for it at an inn met with the reply, 'Petrol! I don't know what it is; I never heard the name before.' On another occasion, however, in the same county, a young woman in an equally remote place at once came forward and produced what was required.

The motorist of those days may have been subject to inconveniences which his modern successor can hardly imagine, but he saw the last of an England that was soon to be a thing of the past, namely the England of Trollope and Whyte-Melville. An early motoring centre, for example, was *Pople's New London Hotel* in Exeter, now hardly a memory in that city.

Finally, during the fourteen years which elapsed between the opening of the century and the outbreak of the First World War, the countryside was dominated, as neither before nor since, by the country-houses, which had not yet become 'stately homes', for their owners lived in, not on, them. They varied, of course, in size, and they varied in respect of the type of parties that were given in them, and it can safely be said that the amount of entertaining done reached its peak during this period. The coming of the motor-car and the improvement in the railway services made it easy to fill them, while their owners were in no way pinched in the pocket, and servants were plentiful and cheap. That these large country-houses and the parties that went on in them

27   King Edward drives with the Kaiser in a Mercedes
while on a visit to Germany in 1906.

brought a good deal of money into the impoverished countryside cannot be denied, but
it is doubtful if they brought much else: society at all levels was still rather rough, and
the sense of humour was everywhere pretty crude.

The outward segregation of the sexes, and the taboo on all that related to their
mutual relations, both a legacy of Victorianism, was a rigid convention, though we now
know that from Royalty and the Cabinet downwards there was very considerable laxity
in the private lives of those who were generally regarded as pillars of society; yet if
a woman of the middle class went in a hansom alone with a man who was neither her
husband nor old enough to be her grandfather her reputation was irretrievably lost.
The ruling convention was directed against unmarried men and women ever being
alone together unless they were engaged, and not always then. If an engagement was
broken off the girl suffered in consequence, while divorce – like cancer – was never
mentioned in polite society.

The British Isles was still the centre of an empire which covered one-fourth of the
land surface of the world, and their inhabitants were supremely conscious of the fact, as
they had shown at the time of the South African War. During the previous decades
there had been a great deal of emigration to the colonies, particularly to Canada,
South Africa, Australia, and New Zealand, and this meant that there were in many
cases close family ties, at all social levels, between the King's subjects at home and those
overseas. Unless this is grasped much of the period will not be understood.

44

3 The European Scene and British Naval Power

THE CONCLUSION of the Anglo-French Entente, with its special provisions relating to Morocco and Egypt, focused attention upon the problems of the Mediterranean, and rarely has the great inland sea played so important a part in the history of mankind as during the decade which culminated in the outbreak of the First World War. Morocco, Bosnia, Herzegovina, Tripoli, and the Balkan Peninsula, all lands whose shores are washed by its waters, are milestones on the road to that struggle.

It will be remembered that the Entente gave France a free hand in Morocco, but her Foreign Minister, Delcassé, made a serious blunder in not conciliating Germany in respect of that country. The goodwill of Italy had been bought by the recognition of her claims to Tripoli, and that of Spain by the hypothetical revision of the northern coastline, but the French government omitted to take any precautions with the only one of its neighbours whom it had serious cause to fear. Bülow determined to make use of this opportunity partly to justify the German contention that Morocco was an international, not a French, concern whatever London and Paris might arrange to the contrary, and partly to test the strength of the Entente. From his point of view the moment was particularly well timed, for, as we shall see, Russia was being beaten by Japan, and was on the eve of revolution; France was torn with dissension over the problem of the separation of Church and State; while in Great Britain the Conservative administration of Balfour was plainly tottering to its fall.

The Kaiser somewhat unwillingly agreed with his Chancellor, and the Moroccan question in a new form may be said to have opened in March 1905, when Wilhelm II landed at Tangier from his yacht, and made a speech to the German colony there in the course of which he said, 'My visit is to show my resolve to do all in my power to safeguard German interests in Morocco. Considering the Sultan is absolutely free, I wish to discuss with him the means to secure these interests.' This was plain enough, but to ensure that there should be no misunderstanding of the German position two introductory sentences were added to the official version of the Imperial speech. 'It is to the Sultan in his capacity of independent sovereign that I pay my visit today. I hope that under his sovereignty a free Morocco will remain open to the peaceful competition of all nations without monopoly or annexation on a policy of absolute equality.' Germany's case, in effect, was that if she did not act Morocco would become a French Protectorate like Tunis, and would be closed to her commerce.

In the early days of April 1905 the Imperial Chancellor took the matter a stage further, and in a circular dispatch suggested a new conference of the signatories of the Treaty of Madrid in 1880, which followed the last international gathering held to discuss the affairs of Morocco. Hardly had this suggestion been made when, under pressure from Germany, the Sultan of Morocco, Abdul Aziz IV, refused to allow his troops to be trained on the French model, and invited the Powers who had signed the Treaty of Madrid to a conference at Tangier. Delcassé was strongly opposed to any such proceeding, but the German government passed from proposals to threats, and as his colleagues were not in the last resort prepared to fight the Foreign Minister resigned at the beginning of June. This was a notable triumph for Germany, though France did not even then give way at once, and it required the intervention of the President of the United States, Theodore Roosevelt, before her consent to the conference was finally secured. 'It looked like war,' he has left on record, 'so I took active hold on the matter though Speck and Jusserand had got things temporarily straightened up. I showed France the great danger of a war, and the little use England could be, and that a conference would not sanction any unjust attack on French interests. I would not accept the invitation unless France was willing, but, if I did, I would, if necessary, take a strong guard against any attitude of Germany which seemed to me unjust and unfair. At last France told me on June 23rd that she would agree.' It was the first decisive intervention of the United States in a European crisis.

The conference met at Algeciras in January 1906, but before then there had been the change of government in London, where Campbell-Bannerman had succeeded Balfour as Prime Minister, and Grey had replaced Lansdowne at the Foreign Office. The substitution of a Liberal administration for a Conservative one, however, had no influence upon the country's foreign policy, and when the French government asked for consultations between their General Staff and the British permission was readily accorded. These military conversations, it may be noted in passing, continued at intervals until 1914, and there were similar, though unofficial, discussions between the British and Belgian Staffs.

The Conference of Algeciras lasted from January to April 1906. The German case was a strong one, for the Treaty of Madrid had ensured every signatory to that document most-favoured-nation status and there was much to be said for the contention of Berlin that this principle extended beyond the economic sphere. What happened, however, was that the German representatives, under the influence of Holstein, over-acted their part, and so alienated the other Powers, though when Bülow realised that Holstein's policy was leading straight to war he took the control out of his hands. A moderating influence was throughout exercised by President Roosevelt, and the Spanish delegates supported their French colleagues, while Austria-Hungary acted as a brake on the German wheel. As for the attitude of Great Britain, it was admirably summed up in an observation of King Edward to the French Ambassador in London, 'Tell us what you said on this point, and we will support you, without restriction or reserve.' Whether London and Madrid were wholly justified in giving Paris this blank cheque is at least arguable.

This Franco-German duel resulted in a draw. It is true that France obtained the control of the Moroccan police for herself and her Spanish ally, but Germany established her contention that the problem of Morocco was the concern of all the Powers. At the same time the conference strengthened the ties between Great Britain and France, while it brought the former into closer touch with Russia who steadily supported her French ally throughout the proceedings. As Professor Gooch has well said, 'The process which Germans describe as encirclement, and Englishmen as insurance, had begun.' For the rest, the part played by Roosevelt was evidence of the increasing importance of the United States as a World Power.

The growing division of the Powers into two camps was, not long after the Conference of Algeciras, followed by the conclusion of an understanding between Great

Britain and Russia. It was only natural that this should be the case, for what kept London and St Petersburg apart was the memory of old rivalries, while the facts of the present, combined with their common alliance with France, were every day tending to bring them together. At the same time agreement was not easy, for there were many outstanding points of difference. In the first place there were British interests in the Persian Gulf which seemed to be threatened by Russia, whose agents, in one disguise or another, swarmed in that area. On the other hand Russian suspicions were roused by British activity in Tibet, and the arrival of the Younghusband Mission in that country in 1904 gave rise to considerable apprehension in St Petersburg. The Russo-Japanese War was also productive of more than one incident between Great Britain and Russia, and war between the two Powers was very close in October 1904, when Russian men-of-war on their way to the Far East opened fire on the Hull fishing fleet on the Dogger Bank.

On the night of the 21st of that month they mistook the British trawlers for Japanese warships, and promptly went into action. A steam trawler was sunk and the captain and third hand killed, while other vessels were severely damaged and some of the crew injured: to render the situation worse the Russian fleet passed on without making the slightest attempt to render any assistance. There was no wireless in those days, and it was not until the 24th that the news of the incident became generally known, causing widespread anger. In the conflict between Russia and Japan public opinion in Britain was overwhelmingly on the side of the latter, and the attack on the Hull fishing fleet added fuel to the fire of popular hatred of Russia. The Tsar tried to pour oil on the troubled waters in a telegram to King Edward VII, who reacted sharply, and for a brief space it looked like war: as in the case of the Fashoda crisis the British Press adopted a very truculent tone, but in the highest circles it was quickly realised that if hostilities did ensue the only party to benefit would be Germany. The Russian government showed no disposition to deny responsibility for the Admiral's mistake, and

28   The Russian outrage on the North Sea fishing fleet,
October 1904. The trawler *Crane* sinks under shell fire,
while the *Gull* stands by to rescue survivors.

29 Russian deputies at a sitting of the Imperial Duma.
Revelations about Rasputin in the Third Duma of 1912
incurred the wrath of the Tsarina, while the Bolsheviks
never acknowledged the Assembly.

Balfour, in spite of the excited state of public feeling, had no intention of proceeding to extremes. Recourse was accordingly had to the Hague Court, which set up an International Commission of Inquiry consisting of British and Russian admirals, together with representatives of the navies of Austria-Hungary, France, and the United States. It met in Paris, and on 25 February 1905 the Commissioners found in favour of Great Britain, condemning Russia to pay £65,000 by way of compensation.

The Russo-Japanese War, of which more hereafter, was generally very unpopular in Russia, and it stimulated the mass of the people to an insurrectionary fervour which brought them into open conflict with the régime. Among the revolutionaries were men, such as Lenin and Trotsky, whose names were to be even better known in years to come, and from end to end of the country there were scenes of violent disorder and bloodshed. The first Russian Revolution, as it has been not inaccurately termed, had in fact been developing ever since the foundation of the Workers' Social Democratic Party in 1898, which five years later split up into the Bolsheviks and the Mensheviks. It was a situation with which Nicholas II soon proved himself quite unfitted to deal. A sentiment of loyalty to his person still existed among the peasantry, and had his character been different he might have won them over to his side. What made the subsequent course of Russian history inevitable took place on 22 January 1905, when an immense deputation of strikers asked permission to present a petition to him at the Winter Palace in St Petersburg: Nicholas refused to leave Tsarskoe Selo, where he had taken refuge, and allowed the petitioning crowd to be shot down by the troops. Neither he nor the monarchy ever recovered the ground which was thus lost.

The internal situation now grew rapidly worse, and mutinies, outbreaks, and repressions became the order of the day: a Soviet of Workers' Deputies was formed in which Trotsky played a prominent part. Such was the opposition from all quarters that the Tsar gave way, and in May 1906 the first Duma, or Parliament, assembled in the Winter Palace, and was opened by Nicholas in person. Between then and the outbreak of the First World War there were several Dumas as the Tsar blew hot and cold, and they usually had a moderate majority of which in happier circumstances advantage might have been taken by the régime. The most capable Prime Minister who emerged was Stolypin, a great advocate of agrarian reform, but in 1911 he was murdered.

The general world situation was not rendered any easier by the fact that the Tsar was as vacillating in international as in domestic affairs. In 1905 the Kaiser was hankering after a return to a more Russophil policy, and he believed that an agreement with St Petersburg would be the most effective reply to the Anglo-French Entente. Accordingly in July of that year he persuaded the Tsar to sign a pact at Björko by which the two Powers agreed that if either of them was attacked by a third European State the other would come to its assistance. When Nicholas returned to his own country he was informed by his Ministers that this agreement conflicted with the terms of the Franco-Russian Alliance, and he was compelled to repudiate it. Shortly afterwards came the Conference of Algeciras, and after somewhat lengthy negotiations Sir Arthur Nicolson and Isvolsky signed, on 31 August 1907, the Anglo-Russian Convention.

The three most important points in this document were those which concerned Persia, Afghanistan, and Tibet. The first of these countries was one of the decaying empires of the Orient with which the West had come into contact, and British and Russian interests were continually clashing in that wide area which was still nominally subject to the Shah. It was now agreed to divide Persia into a large Russian and a small British sphere of influence, with a neutral zone between them in which the two Powers were to be on an equal footing. The Persian Gulf was not mentioned since it was only partly in the Shah's dominions, but Grey emphasised the intention of the British

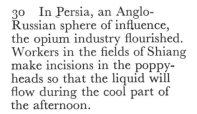

30 In Persia, an Anglo-Russian sphere of influence, the opium industry flourished. Workers in the fields of Shiang make incisions in the poppy-heads so that the liquid will flow during the cool part of the afternoon.

49

government to maintain the *status quo* in that quarter. So far as Afghanistan was concerned Great Britain declared that she had no intention of interfering in its internal concerns, and she promised neither herself to take, nor to encourage the Amir to take, any measures threatening Russia. The Russian government, on its part, recognised Afghanistan as outside its sphere of influence, and promised that all its political relations with Kabul should be conducted through the British Foreign Office. In the matter of Tibet the two Powers agreed to respect its territorial integrity, and to abstain from all interference in its internal administration.

The reconciliation of Great Britain and Russia was confirmed by the conclusion of an understanding between their respective allies. In June 1907 France and Japan had already agreed not to take any steps contrary to the independence and integrity of China, and in the following month Russia and Japan signed a similar treaty, by which they agreed to maintain the *status quo*, and to secure respect for it by all pacific means at their disposal. Three months later they signed a further instrument that disposed of several problems left over from the Treaty of Portsmouth which had concluded the war between them.

The conclusion of these various arrangements did much to redress the balance which had been upset in Germany's favour by the Japanese victory in the Russo-Japanese War, though this fact was not appreciated in all circles in Berlin. Russia, having relinquished her ambitions in the Far East, and having accepted her defeat by Japan, was now able once more to turn to the Balkans and the West. As for Japan, her hands were now completely free, and she set to work to build up that commanding position in eastern Asia which was to be so prominent a feature of the years to come; a position to which she never could have attained had it not been that the quarrels of the European Powers on their own continent compelled them to relax that grip on the Orient which they had established during the previous century and a half. Tribute is certainly due to Grey for his courage in coming to an agreement with Russia, for, like

31 Admiral Togo, commander of the Japanese fleet during the Russo-Japanese War and later Chief of the Japanese Naval Staff.

50

George Canning in an earlier day, he had to carry out his foreign policy in spite of a section of opinion in his own party, some Liberals, and a great many Socialists, being opposed to the particular type of autocracy which then existed in Russia. A few Conservatives, too, disapproved of the concessions which had been made in the Middle East; yet the Anglo-Russian Convention did much to save Europe seven years later, for it ensured that when Germany fought she should from the beginning have to do so on two fronts. In this respect the contrast with 1939 is instructive.

Meanwhile the growth of the German navy had long been watched with envious eyes at the British Admiralty. In Britain at that time the navy was in no way a party question, for it was common knowledge that the protection of the country's food supplies in time of war was dependent on the possession of sea power, and that the existence of the British Empire itself rested in the last resort on the ability of the British fleet to keep the seas against its enemies. As a rough guide to an Admiralty practice, it was part of the national policy to aim at a Two-Power standard, that is to say a navy capable of dealing effectively with the navies of the two next strongest naval Powers in the world. The growth of German naval aspirations modified the whole situation, and German naval policy was seen as a definite menace. At whatever sacrifice Britain must outbuild her new rival, and in 1904 the first steps were taken to redress a balance which was no longer in her favour.

The motive force was Sir John Fisher, who had entered the navy in 1854 at the age of thirteen, and at the turn of the century he was Commander-in-Chief in the Mediterranean. Two years later he was recalled to the Admiralty as Second Sea Lord, and in that capacity he quickly made his reforming zeal felt. He devised a new system of naval education, and sketched out a scheme for rendering the fleet an effective weapon of war which should be ready to strike at a moment's notice. At his own request he was in 1903 transferred from the post of Second Sea Lord to that of Commander-in-Chief at Portsmouth, but while he held that office he was also busily engaged in drafting further plans for the reorganisation of the country's fighting forces; nor was he by any means content with his own Service, for he readily accepted a seat on the Esher Committee whose task it was to reform the War Office.

Fisher was a very remarkable man, and his physical exuberance developed into literary and controversial profusion; he spoke, wrote, and thought in large type and italics; when writing he underlined his argument with two, three, or even four strokes with a broad-nibbed pen, and when talking with blows of his fist on the palm of his other hand. 'I wish you would stop shaking your fist in my face,' King Edward VII said to him on one occasion when being subjected to one of his more forceful arguments. Fisher never played field games or indulged in any form of athletics, and the only exercise he took was walking. This distaste for sport may have originated in the fact that in his younger days he had shot a butler in mistake for a rabbit, though his only recorded comment on the incident was that 'he was a pompous old fellow and it did him good'.

In the course of 1904, largely under his inspiration, a reform in the distribution and methods of mobilisation of the fleet was put into practice, and in view of the growing rivalry with Germany concentration was its keynote. Fisher took the opportunity of this reorganisation to effect a redistribution of British men-of-war over the world in order to meet the altered conditions of the day. The policy was to make the squadrons on foreign

32 Admiral Sir John Fisher (1841-1920). He retired from the Admiralty in January 1910, but was recalled as First Sea Lord in October 1914. At his death he was regarded as the greatest British sailor since Nelson.

stations more efficient and less vulnerable, while permitting the strengthening of the Home Fleet without any serious increase in the Naval Estimates. Fisher characteristically described his scheme in a letter as 'Napoleonic in its audacity and Cromwellian in its thoroughness', and added that unless naval reform was 'ruthless and remorseless . . . we may as well pack up and hand over to Germany'.

All gunboats were withdrawn except those necessary for river service in China and on the west coast of Africa. The ships stationed permanently on the south-east coast of the American continent were withdrawn, and this coast was in future merely to be visited annually by other ships. The Pacific Squadron was also withdrawn, with the exception of one vessel to police the Bering Sea seal-fishing. The China, Australia, and East India squadrons were formed entirely of cruisers, and, although retained as separate commands, their respective admirals or commanders met periodically to discuss the problems of their stations, and to arrange for joint action in the event of war. As it was now imperative to keep the maximum number of ships in the Channel the old Home Fleet was increased to fourteen battleships, together with six armoured cruisers, as well as a proportion of light cruisers and destroyers, and it was renamed the Channel Fleet.

The Mediterranean Fleet was fixed at nine battleships, with four armoured cruisers, smaller cruisers, and destroyers; while a third Fleet, based on Gibraltar, was formed, to act as a reinforcement either in the Channel or in the Mediterranean; this was given the name of the Atlantic Fleet, and was composed of nine battleships with six armoured cruisers and various smaller ships. Finally, a new Cruiser Squadron was

33 The first H.M.S. *Dreadnought*. Dimensions: length (overall), 526 feet, beam, 82 feet, draught (maximum), 31 feet. Displacement, about 20,700 tons (full load). Guns: ten 12-inch; 27 12-pounders. Speed, 21 knots. The ship was built, in Portsmouth Dockyard, in a year and a day.

formed of six ships, and was to be used for training purposes in time of peace; it was intended that this Squadron should show the flag at the West Indian ports and on the coast of South America, while in wartime it was to join the Channel or Mediterranean Fleet as might be required. The new organisation was designed to give a 10 per cent superiority over a combination either of France and Russia, or of Germany and Russia, the United States not being regarded seriously as a naval Power at that time.

Great economies were effected by the abolition of unnecessary and obsolete ships on foreign stations, but, in addition, the withdrawal of these craft rendered several subsidiary dockyards useless, and here again money was saved. The naval bases at Halifax, Jamaica, St Lucia, Ascension, and Esquimault were abolished, though at Ascension a sufficient force of marines was maintained to man the guns in order to prevent the anchorage being used by an enemy in wartime. The base at Trincomalee was closed. The base on the China station, on the other hand, was expanded as circumstances required, and that at Gibraltar was enlarged so as to cope with the refits of the Atlantic Fleet, for it was assumed that in war Gibraltar would be a valuable repair base between England and Malta.

As may be supposed this reorganisation caused a good deal of controversy, and Fisher's leading opponent was another admiral, Lord Charles Beresford, at that time Commander-in-Chief of the Channel Fleet. Whatever Fisher proposed Beresford opposed, and Sir Winston Churchill has left it on record that 'the lamentable situation thus created might easily have ruined the discipline of the Navy, but for the fact that a third large body of officers resolutely refused, at whatever cost to themselves, to participate in the struggle'. It may be added that in all his reforms Fisher had the steady backing of the King for whom he entertained feelings bordering on veneration, while the monarch also had a very high regard for the admiral.

The return of a Liberal administration to office in 1906 altered neither the pace nor the direction of British naval policy, and among the earlier steps of the new government was the launching of the first *Dreadnought* and the concentration of the Home Fleet in the North Sea. The *Dreadnought* rendered all other battleships in the world virtually obsolete, and so went a long way to reduce the superiority which the British navy enjoyed over the German. The Germans responded by a new Navy Law, and henceforth the race of naval armaments was open and unconcealed, while it certainly did not escape the notice of the British Admiralty that the heavily armour-plated High Sea Fleet was constructed not for distant voyages but for a conflict with a strong opponent in the North Sea.

In retrospect it is easy to see that the cause of this calamitous competition was mutual suspicion: in particular the German Emperor and his advisers were fearful that Britain might launch a preventive war while their navy was still relatively weak, and therefore national security demanded that it should be strengthened as rapidly as possible. From this premise it followed that the more ships Germany laid down the sooner a preventive war would become impracticable, and so the more quickly she would impress her rival. In these circumstances any suggestion from London that there should be an agreed limitation which would leave Britain with a naval preponderance was regarded askance in Berlin, and when Sir Charles Hardinge, in August 1908, made a suggestion along these lines at Cranberg, the Kaiser himself told him that he would rather go to war.

34   Lord Charles Beresford (*centre; see p. 53*) with his guests at a House of Commons point-to-point in 1910. Note the style of clothes favoured by England's richer women.

4 The Awakening of the Far East

AS THE NINETEENTH CENTURY drew to its close the problems of the Far East began to assume a world-wide importance which had not been theirs since those far-off days when the course of events in China more than once set forces in motion which eventually overturned empires in Europe. There is a regrettable tendency to regard international relations over too short a period, and the result of this has often been to obscure the fact that when the West came into contact with the East in the eighteenth and nineteenth centuries Asia was undergoing one of its periods of decline while Europe was in the ascendant. It had not always been so, and for several hundreds of years previously the West had been on the defensive, for the Arabs had crossed the Pyrenees into France and the Turks had twice besieged Vienna. Now, however, the Ottoman and Persian monarchies were decadent, and the Chinese Empire was in a similar condition. That this state of affairs might not be permanent, and represented but one cycle among many, never seems to have occurred to the statesmen of contemporary Europe; their successors in our own day have in consequence been compelled to learn the lesson in a hard school.

For many centuries the great nation of the Far East was, to the outside world, China, and it was in no way surprising that this should have been the case. In 1662 the last of the native Ming emperors committed suicide, and henceforth the destinies of the Chinese Empire were in the hands of the victorious Manchu invaders. The earlier monarchs of this dynasty were men of great force of character, perhaps the most noteworthy being K'en Ho (1662–1723) and Ch'ien Lung (1736–96): with the death of the latter decay set in. It is to be noted that the Manchus ruled not only over China proper but also over vast territories which have since, temporarily or permanently, passed into other hands, such as Tibet and Turkestan: Manchu armies penetrated Burma; and Korea, Annam, and Siam paid tribute to Pekin. During this period there were many contacts, both commercial and cultural, with Europe, and the influence of France, then at the zenith of her power, was felt in the Far East. Louis XIV took a personal interest in Oriental matters, and the splendour of Versailles can easily be traced among the ruins of the Summer Palace in Pekin. The Manchus reciprocated: Jesuits were placed in charge of the bureau of astronomy; and K'ang Hsi issued what amounted to an edict of religious toleration.

For many years all went well, for although the Chinese had a rooted dislike of foreigners the Manchus were foreigners themselves, and by no means shared all the prejudices of their subjects: Ch'ien Lung, for example, treated the British Ambassador, Lord Macartney, with perfect courtesy, but after his death the Manchu grip slackened. Down the ages the Chinese have always shown a tendency to conquer their conquerors, as exemplified by the fact that when the Manchus conquered the country they imposed the pigtail on the Chinese as a badge of servitude, yet before long they were wearing it themselves. Relations with Europe deteriorated, largely owing to the attitude of superiority affected by the Chinese in their dealings with the outside world; they

35   The sleeping apartments of the Dowager Empress Tzu-Hsi in the new Summer
Palace at Pekin. This palace was built in 1894, when the Dowager Empress
appropriated a huge sum meant for the building of a modern navy.

refused to treat on any basis of equality, and regarded all foreign envoys as bearers of
tribute, with the result that an impossible state of affairs came into existence. By the
beginning of the nineteenth century Canton was the only port open to merchants from
abroad; the Europeans there were confined to a small area, and were ordered to spend
the quiet months of each year at the neighbouring Portuguese possession of Macao. Nor
was this all, for there were many other vexatious regulations, such as the absence of
fixed tariff charges, the exactions of corrupt officials, the prohibition against a Chinese
teaching a foreigner the language, and the subjection of Europeans to the jurisdiction
of the Chinese courts.

These pretensions were not supported by any real military power, or capacity. The
Chinese of those days were a peace-loving people who held soldiers in low esteem, and
the Manchu garrisons, which had been placed in the principal cities, were far from
being distinguished by that warlike spirit which had animated their ancestors two
centuries earlier: their arms were also markedly inferior to those of European troops.
Furthermore, there was a want of cohesion about the whole Chinese Empire. The
Manchus had left the provinces a considerable amount of autonomy, and particularism
was the keynote of both civil and military administration. To quote a British representative at Pekin,

> If the Governor-General of Canton got into difficulties with the English, if his forts
> were captured, his war-junks destroyed, and the city itself forced to pay a heavy
> ransom as the price of being spared an assault, his immediate neighbour, the Governor-
> General of Funkien, did not regard it as his duty to render assistance, or even to abstain
> from friendly relations with the English, and Cantonese willingly enrolled themselves

to carry the scaling ladders for the English troops which took by assault the forts at the mouth of the river that was the highway to Pekin.

Such being the case opportunities for aggression on one side, for obstruction on the other, and for misunderstanding on both, abounded, and the European Powers proceeded often by force of arms to press their wishes upon the Chinese who were compelled to open their ports to foreign trade. Legations were established in Pekin by all the leading Powers, and this betokened a changed attitude in their relations with China. Hitherto they had tended in the main to settle disputes, peaceably or otherwise, with local officials, but they now began to treat with the Imperial government direct. This development, of course, implied that the Imperial government could make its will effective throughout the whole Empire; this was certainly not the case, since for many years after 1851 there had been in progress the Taiping Rebellion, which was in part organised banditry and in part a nationalist rising against the Manchus. The foreign Powers now proceeded to assist the Imperial government to suppress the Taipings, and largely owing to the strategy of the British General Gordon this was accomplished by the summer of 1864, but not before the richest provinces of the Empire had been devastated by civil war for upwards of a decade. As the nineteenth century drew to its close, therefore, everything pointed to the fact that China was on the eve of another of those periods of weakness which have occurred so often during her long history. The dynasty was in full decay; the country was weakened by internal strife; and the Imperial government had lost prestige in consequence of the concessions which it had been compelled to make to foreign Powers. At this point another rival appeared upon the scene in the shape of Japan.

This is not the place for an account of the earlier Japanese relations with the outside world, for ever since 1638 these had been non-existent except for the fact that a few Dutch and Chinese traders had been tolerated, rather than encouraged, at Nagasaki: Japanese subjects, it may be added, were forbidden to travel or to trade abroad. The position was further complicated by the fact that for six and a half centuries the legitimate sovereign, that is to say the Mikado, had been a mere figure-head: he kept entirely in the background, exercised no authority whatever, and was never seen by the people. He was surrounded by a sort of phantom Court, whose members bore administrative titles dating from the remote period when he was a real as well as a nominal ruler. All effective power was in the hands of an individual called the Shogun or Tycoon.

More than once during the earlier years of the nineteenth century attempts had been made by the European Powers to persuade the Shogun to adopt a different attitude towards foreigners, but without success, and it was not until the arrival of U.S. Commodore Perry with his squadron in 1853 that a new policy began to be adopted. Thereafter events moved rapidly: the Shogunate was overthrown in 1868, the Mikado resumed the powers of which he had been divested for centuries, and Japan appeared in due course with a constitution modelled on that of the German Empire. Needless to say, these developments were not uninfluenced by what was taking place in contemporary China. Japanese statesmen realised that whether the Orient liked it or not the Europeans and Americans had come to stay, and the results of the obstructionist policy of the Chinese government were not encouraging. The Mikado and his advisers, therefore, decided to adopt quite another line, and to allow their country to be

MAP NO. 3 THE FAR EAST

58

36   Japanese court ceremonial in 1912. Bows and arrows
are carried at the funeral of the Mikado of Japan, Meiji, in
Tokyo. The soldiers and sailors wear Western-style
uniforms, a result of the emperor's modernising policy.

Westernised, at any rate externally, in the hope that by this means she might not only
be able to retain her independence, but also to take advantage of the increasing
embarrassment of her Chinese enemy and neighbour.

The affairs of Korea soon provided both an opportunity and an excuse for Japanese
expansion. That country was in the anomalous position of being tributary to two
separate Powers, China and Japan, and so long ago as the seventeenth century it had
got into difficulty with the Chinese Emperor on the question of suzerainty. By the end
of the nineteenth century Korea was in a state bordering on anarchy, and Tokyo
pressed for reforms of which Pekin would not hear. When the Japanese took the matter
up with the Korean government direct China began to prepare for war, and by the
summer of 1894 hostilities had broken out. It was universally assumed that China, with
her vast resources, would overwhelm her tiny rival, and great was the astonishment
throughout the world when this did not prove to be the case. The armies and fleets of
the Celestial Empire went down to disaster before those of Dai Nippon, and the
consequences of this were seen in the Treaty of Shimonoseki which was signed in
April 1895. By this treaty the Chinese ceded to Japan the Liao-Tung Peninsula, the
island of Formosa, and the Pescadores group of islands, while there was also an
indemnity.

The balance of power in the Far East had clearly shifted, and before long this
change was destined to have the most momentous consequences all over the world. It
is difficult to decide whether the Powers were more surprised or displeased. Russia had

no desire to have as a neighbour an aggressive Japan rather than a moribund China; France was apprehensive of anything that might weaken her Russian ally; while Germany did not want to see Russia turning to Europe in consequence of being thwarted in Asia. On the other hand, if China was really so weak as she had proved herself to be in the recent war then she was in no condition to resist any demands which might be made upon her from other quarters.

With these considerations in mind the governments of France, Germany, and Russia presented a collective note to Japan urging her to forgo the acquisition of the Liao-Tung Peninsula on the ground that whoever possessed Port Arthur, the great fortress at the tip of it, would dominate Pekin. The Japanese very wisely gave way, and secured a further monetary payment by way of recompense. The sum was lent to China by Germany and Russia, who thereby strengthened their hold on the Pekin government. With Japan thus out of the way the three Powers proceeded to put pressure upon the helpless Chinese. The result from their point of view was all that could be desired. In 1897 Germany obtained one of the best ports in the Far East at Tsingtao, though owing to her weakness at sea she in reality held it by courtesy of Great Britain and Japan. The following year saw Russia established in Port Arthur from which the Japanese had been requested to withdraw, while France demanded the port of Kwang Chow Wen, and accepted an assurance from the Chinese government that the *hinterland* would be recognised as being under French influence. In 1898, too, Great Britain obtained a base at Wei-Hai-Wei, though this was not regarded by Japan as an unfriendly act, since the British government had manifested its friendship for Tokyo four years before by the surrender of extra-territorial rights in that country; it had also refused to be associated with the collective note of France, Germany, and Russia.

The attitude adopted by Russia at this time is understandable; her energies were concentrated on the Far East, and she was not prepared to tolerate a rival there, even if she had to fight. Germany, on the other hand, was not vitally affected by recent

37   The Dowager Empress (1835–1908) waves her handkerchief to the wives of European diplomats. Her strong will and reactionary policies kept the ramshackle Empire of China together, but her greed, and her encouragement of the Boxer rebellion, did nothing to help China.

60

developments, and her deliberate alienation of Japan was all of a piece with that reckless giving of pledges to fortune which had marked her policy ever since the fall of Bismarck. Russia was no longer her friend, so it was an act of folly to antagonise Russia's potential enemy, Japan, as she was to realise on the outbreak of the First World War.

The Japanese government was far from forgetting the affront which it had received, but events in China for a time concentrated foreign attention upon the internal policies of that country. An attempt at reform under the auspices of the weak, but well-meaning, Emperor Kwang Hsi was prevented by the Dowager Empress, who then endeavoured to distract attention from abuses at home by encouragement of the ultra-nationalist Boxers – in many ways the spiritual heirs of the Taipings – whose Chinese name means 'patriotic harmonious fists'. This policy succeeded so well that before long the lives of foreigners were unsafe, and the legations in Pekin were besieged. An international force was dispatched to the Far East in 1900, and the rivalries of the Powers were suspended while they came to the aid of their fellow countrymen. When the Boxers had been crushed, China was called upon to pay the price, which proved to be no light one. Two Imperial princes were sentenced to death, three high officials were ordered to commit suicide, and three leading Mandarins were beheaded; in addition missions were sent to Berlin and Tokyo to present the Chinese Emperor's apologies for the murders of German and Japanese diplomats; lastly there was an indemnity of 450,000,000 Taels. The result of the Boxer Rising was thus to impose further burdens on China, while the terms of the Powers caused the dynasty to lose face to such an extent that its overthrow became a mere question of time.

This settlement was reached in September 1901 and in January of the following year the Anglo-Japanese Agreement, as it was called, though it was really a defensive alliance, was concluded for a period of five years. Relations between the two countries had, as we have seen, always been friendly, and both had recently experienced the

38   A headsman with sword stands with Chinese troops and officials at the eastern entrance to the Forbidden City in Pekin. This entrance was used only by European diplomats visiting the Imperial Palace.

61

39 Boxer prisoners, their heads through boards, are led in
by a Sikh soldier of the International force. Boxers attacked
foreigners and Chinese Christians; diplomatic immunity was
violated (the German minister murdered) and the legation
quarter of Pekin besieged.

dangers of isolation, so it was not unnatural that they should come together. By the
agreement they recognised the independence of China and Korea; but they authorised
each other to safeguard their special interests in those countries by intervention if they
were threatened either by the aggression of another Power or by internal disturbances.
If either Britain or Japan in the defence of such interests became involved in war the
other would maintain strict neutrality; if, however, either were to be at war with two
Powers, its partner would come to its assistance.

In the existing state of international politics this treaty afforded equal cause for
satisfaction to both the parties to it. Great Britain, faced by the increasing naval
strength of Germany, was able to leave the Pacific waters to the care of her new ally,
and herself to concentrate on the North Sea and the Atlantic. Her statesmen also
entertained the hope, destined to be disappointed, that in alliance with Japan they
would be able to restrain her ambitions more easily than might otherwise have proved
to be the case. As for Japan, her prestige throughout the East was greatly enhanced by
the fact that she was the first Oriental State in modern times to conclude an agreement
with a European Power upon equal terms, while the substance of the treaty afforded her
every assurance that when she had to fight Russia she would have a clear field.

That hour was clearly approaching, for Russian influence was penetrating northern
China at an accelerated pace: not only was St Petersburg pouring troops into Manchuria
but permission was obtained from Pekin to make railways connecting Vladivostok and

Port Arthur with the Siberian system. The winter of 1902–3 was marked by fresh activities on the part of Russian subjects in North Korea, and by the movement of Russian troops towards the Yalu River under pretext of protecting nationals who were cutting timber there in right of a concession from the Chinese government. Japan had always been as sensitive concerning foreign interference in Korea as has Great Britain in respect of the position in the Low Countries, and for the same reason, namely the threat to her own shores, so her government at once took alarm: lengthy negotiations between St Petersburg and Tokyo then ensued, and they culminated in January 1904 in a Japanese promise to regard Manchuria as outside Japan's sphere of influence if Russia would give a similar undertaking in respect of Korea. No reply was received within the period considered sufficient by the Japanese, that is to say three weeks, and diplomatic relations with Russia were promptly severed.

Once more it was generally assumed that Japan must inevitably be defeated, as her resources were vastly smaller than those of her antagonist, while Russian military prestige stood very high indeed; above all, nearly four centuries had elapsed since an Oriental Power had defeated a Western, and the memory of the Turkish victories in the sixteenth century had grown very dim. What was widely ignored was that the Japanese land and naval forces were thoroughly ready for the contest. The army had been greatly expanded, reorganised, and re-equipped since the war with China, and could put into the field a force far greater than the Russians believed possible. The navy was composed of six battleships and eight armoured cruisers, with numerous smaller cruisers, and torpedo craft, and was an homogeneous, efficient, and ably organised force, manned by a well-trained and zealous personnel. Japan, further, had the great advantage of being close to the theatre of war, whereas the main Russian military and naval centres were far away, and Russia could maintain only a portion of her forces in the Far East, and had great difficulty in reinforcing them. Nor was this all, for the Russian army was poorly led and indifferently trained, and this was even more true of the navy.

40 A Japanese field-battery in action before Port Arthur. The Japanese siege lasted from summer 1904 until January 1905, when the Russian commander treacherously sent out the white flag, even though the garrison was well provisioned.

63

Both parties were weak financially: the Japanese relied on London and New York for war loans, while Russia borrowed chiefly from her French ally.

The war was a record of successes for Japan. Her army took Port Arthur after a terrible and costly siege, defeated the Russian field armies in the battles of Liaoyang and the Shaho, and in the great three weeks' contest around Mukden from 20 February to 10 March 1905 in which nearly 700,000 men were involved. The Japanese navy, under the brilliant leadership of Admiral Togo, utterly destroyed Russian sea power by bottling up the Pacific fleet in Port Arthur, where most of the units were captured on the surrender of the fortress: a second fleet was sent out from the Baltic, and, as we have seen, nearly precipitated war with Great Britain on the way, but Togo inflicted upon it the most crushing defeat that modern naval history records in the Battle of Tsushima, on 27 to 28 May. Perhaps the most apposite comment on the war was that of Sir Frederick Maurice:

> The success of Japan cannot be ascribed to the greater valour of the troops. Splendid as was the courage of the Japanese soldiery, the Russians, whom no glimmer of success had come to cheer, fought with a dogged determination which commands equal respect. . . . The national spirit of Russia had never fired her armies or fleets, nor singleness of purpose inspired her leaders. Japan had been victorious because she had learnt from her German tutors that war is the business, not merely of the soldier or of the sailor, but of the nation as a whole.

If the Japanese knew how to make war they also knew when to make peace, and by the summer of 1905 they had shot their bolt. They had gained the objectives for which they commenced the conflict, but their heavy losses in man-power were beginning to tell upon the strength of their armies: furthermore, Japan was at the end of her financial resources, and was finding it increasingly difficult to raise fresh loans. Although Russia was also in desperate straits financially, and faced with growing unrest, her armies had not been decisively defeated, and her vast resources in men were hardly affected even by the heavy casualties her forces had sustained. Mediation prospects, too, were being canvassed in some quarters in Europe, and although Japan was saved by her alliance with Great Britain from a repetition of the events of 1895 her government decided not to run any risks. Accordingly, at the end of May 1905, they secretly asked the President of the United States, Theodore Roosevelt, to mediate, and in consequence he sent an invitation to the belligerents to a peace conference in his country, which was duly accepted. A settlement was quickly reached, and peace between Japan and Russia was concluded by the Treaty of Portsmouth, New Hampshire, on 5 September 1905.

By this settlement Russia acknowledged the paramount interests of Japan in Korea, and agreed not to obstruct any measures which the Japanese might take there; she transferred to Japan, subject to Chinese consent, her lease of Liao-Tung and the southern branch of the Chinese Eastern Railway from Port Arthur to Changchun; and she also ceded the southern half of the island of Sakhalin. Both Powers agreed to withdraw their armies from Manchuria, and not to interfere with any measures which China might take for her industrial and commercial development. Russia further denied that she possessed any exclusive rights in Manchuria inconsistent with the 'Open Door' policy, and both Powers declared that they would not use their railways there

64

41   Russian troops on the Eastern front get a heavy 6-inch
Howitzer gun into position.

for strategic purposes with the exception of those based on the Liao-Tung zone.

From whatever angle it be regarded the Treaty of Portsmouth must appear as one of the great events of modern history, for it would be impossible to exaggerate its importance. Its effect upon the Tsarist régime in Russia was comparable with that of the Boxer Rising upon the Manchu dynasty in China; defeat in the field led to rebellion at home, and although this was suppressed for a time the seeds had been sown of the Revolution of 1917. The connection between the Treaty of Portsmouth and the establishment of Bolshevism is much closer than has always been realised; moreover, it was the proved incompetence of the Tsarist régime which produced both. If defeat had serious consequences within Russia it had the gravest repercussions outside the country; the Muscovite colossus was proved to have feet of clay, and the fact was duly noted in Berlin. The balance of power was affected, and the aggressive elements in Germany were led to the conclusion that a war on two fronts might not be such a formidable proposition after all; even if Britain did join in, so it was argued, that would not make a great deal of difference in view of her ineptitude in the South African War. So the treaty which was concluded in New Hampshire in August 1905 had a direct bearing upon the course of events in another August nine years later.

In Asia the results were not less striking. An Eastern nation had beaten a European in fair fight, and every Oriental felt that the tide had turned at last. From the Treaty of Portsmouth dates not only the belief by Japan in her destiny as the mistress of Asia, but the rise of nationalism in Turkey, Persia, India, and many another country. Some years, indeed, were to pass before these developments were to make themselves felt in all their

65

intensity, but when they did it was clearly seen that they had their origin in the Treaty of Portsmouth.

Japanese policy soon left no doubt that in the eyes of Tokyo the treaty was a beginning, not an end. Already on 12 August a new Treaty of Alliance had been signed with Great Britain, though it was not made public until after the close of the war with Russia. Its objects were, on the British side, to dissuade the Russians from any idea of recouping their losses in the Far East by an advance in Central Asia, and, on the part of Japan, to clear the way for complete Japanese control in Korea. The aims of the Alliance were stated to be the preservation of peace in Eastern Asia and India; the maintenance of the independence and territorial integrity of the Chinese Empire and of the 'Open Door' there; and the defence of the territorial rights and special interests of Japan and Great Britain in the regions specified. Should either Power be involved in war in upholding those rights and interests the other was now bound to come immediately to its aid. Furthermore, Great Britain recognised the paramount interests of Japan in Korea and her right to take what measures she thought best to protect them; and Japan recognised a similar right on the part of Great Britain in the Indian frontier region.

This agreement was speedily followed up by one with Korea, on 17 November, by which Japan assumed complete control of the foreign affairs of that country, and appointed a Resident-General at Seoul, the capital, with subordinates in the other more important centres of population. The first Resident-General was Prince Ito, who secured a free hand in spite of the opposition of the militarists, now beginning to make their influence felt as a result of two victorious wars; he appears sincerely to have cherished the hope that under his guidance Korea would make such progress as would ensure her eventual ability to stand alone. If he entertained such expectations he was doomed to disappointment, partly because of the opposition of a native official class

42   10 March 1905. The Russian army leaves Mukden in flames. In this battle, the greatest of the war, 89,000 Russians and 71,000 Japanese were killed. The Russian General Kuropatkin successfully drew off his remaining troops to the north.

opposed to all reform, and partly because of the hostility aroused among the mass of the people by the overbearing, and unscrupulous, conduct of many of the Japanese who came to Korea to advance their fortunes. Prince Ito was eventually murdered by a Korean in 1909, but even before that events were moving swiftly in the direction of annexation. In 1907 Russia agreed to this, and three years later Great Britain did so, with the result that on 22 August 1910 Korea was annexed by Japan, and the Japanese government undertook to maintain the existing tariff rates for another decade.

Simultaneously Japan pursued a forward policy where China was concerned, for the victory over Russia had brought her into Manchuria. By the Treaty of Pekin of 22 December 1905 China agreed to the terms of the Portsmouth settlement so far as they affected her, and by a Sino-Japanese agreement of the same date she consented to the opening of sixteen towns in Manchuria to foreign trade and residence, and to the reconstruction by Japan of the light railway built during the war to connect Antung, on the Korean frontier, with Mukden: Japan was to have the right to operate the line for fifteen years from the completion of the improvements to it, but a good deal of friction ensued, which included an ultimatum from Tokyo to Pekin, before the work of reconstruction was finished in 1911.

Railways, it is to be observed, and the South Manchurian Railway Company in particular, were among the more important means of Japanese expansion in Manchuria at this time as Japan proceeded steadily to consolidate and extend her rights there. The Chinese were too weak to take any overt step to resist this, but they endeavoured to check it by granting railway concessions to British and American interests in the hope of embroiling Japan with Great Britain and the United States. This ingenious scheme, however, came to nothing, for London supported Tokyo, and in July 1907 Japan and Russia drew together, and concluded a secret treaty which defined their respective spheres of interest in Manchuria, recognised Russian special rights in Mongolia, and agreed to Japanese domination of Korea. In 1909 the United States did take the initiative in the Far East, but it only served to show that she was still a long way from being a World Power: her proposal was that China should be given an international loan to enable her to purchase the foreign-controlled Manchurian railways and so to ensure their neutralisation, but Russia and Japan united in rejecting the scheme, while Great Britain and France supported their respective allies. The only result of this essay in diplomacy was to bring Russia and Japan closer together.

Meanwhile relations between Japan and the United States were also becoming more strained over the subject of immigration, and there was a good deal of talk about the possibility of war between them. Such a development would have been as harmful to British interests as it would have been beneficial to German, and this fact was duly noted in Tokyo: accordingly, when in 1910 Great Britain approached Japan on the subject of reconciling the Alliance with a Treaty of General Arbitration which she expected to conclude with the United States she found the Japanese government perfectly willing to consent to such a revision. The result was the third Anglo-Japanese Treaty of Alliance in 1911, which omitted all mention of Korea and the Indian frontier, since, as we have seen, Russia was now the friend of both parties; but it was provided that if either ally concluded an arbitration treaty with a third Power, the Anglo-Japanese Alliance was not to be operative against that Power.

If the opening years of the twentieth century had seen Japan going on from strength to strength the opposite had been the case where China was concerned. In November 1908 there died the Emperor Kwang Hsi, who in happier circumstances might have been able to effect the necessary reforms, and he was followed to the grave by the Dowager Empress, who had strictly opposed any reform at all. The new Emperor, Hsuan Tung, was an infant of two, and it was clear to all that the end was at hand. The whole machinery of government was everywhere breaking down, and the provinces were in revolt on all sides, though it is to be noted that the movement against the Court at this stage was more anti-dynastic than republican. Finally, in 1912, the transition from the Manchu régime was effected under the auspices of Yuan Shih-Kai, though it was by no means certain that this was anything more than a stage in the transition to a new dynasty founded by Yuan Shih-Kai himself.

Such was the state of the Far East when the First World War broke out, and this event was hailed by the rulers of Japan as a golden opportunity to secure hegemony over China.

43　The Russian fleet at Port Arthur. Russia had gained the port from China in 1897 – as an ice-free port for its Pacific Fleet. In 1905 it was transferred to the Japanese.

5 Turkey, the Balkans, and North Africa

IT HAS ALREADY BEEN SHOWN that at the beginning of the nineteenth century Turkey was moribund, but it still stretched over a large area in Europe, Asia, and Africa, as a glance at the map will show. The last general settlement of affairs in the Near East had been at the Treaty of Berlin in 1878, and there had been little change since then except that to all intents and purposes Egypt had passed under British rule. The Christian States in the Balkans were vigorous enough, but they showed little tendency to combine, while the Turks were in no condition to take advantage of these centrifugal tendencies, for no serious effort was made by the Porte to set its house in order, and the Ottoman Empire continued to decay.

During these years, however, there was a marked change in the attitude of the Powers individually towards the Near East and its problems. Salisbury as leader of the Conservative Party in Britain by no means shared the Turcophil sentiments of his predecessor, Disraeli, and from 1885 onwards there was little difference in viewpoint between the two British parties where international affairs were concerned: the result was that the period was marked by much greater consistency in British foreign policy than had been the case for several decades, and in the Near East it was consistently anti-Turk. Not the least important reason for this was that Turkey no longer played a vital part in the British line of communications with India, the Far East, and Australasia. The possession of Cyprus, acquired by the Treaty of Berlin, and of Egypt had completely transformed the situation, and a strong Ottoman Empire was not an essential factor in the strategy of the British Empire; furthermore, Turkish methods of government had never commended themselves to the British public, and now that there was no need to wink at them for political reasons they aroused positive disgust.

The policy of Russia, too, underwent modification. Her experiences in Bulgaria in the eighties of the nineteenth century, when she had received little thanks for championing that country against the Turks, had disgusted her with the affairs of South-East Europe, and her rulers' attention was increasingly attracted by the Far East, where another dying empire – the Chinese – seemed to offer greater prizes. This dream, it is true, was shattered by the Treaty of Portsmouth, but after that St Petersburg tended to be interested in the Middle, rather than in the Near, East; that is to say in Persia rather than in Turkey. For all these reasons the scene at Constantinople was changed. Ottoman rights were no longer fiercely challenged by Russia and hotly defended by Great Britain. For thirty-six years Turk and Muscovite did not cross swords, and when war once more broke out between them both found themselves in company which would have been inconceivable a generation before.

While the older combatants were withdrawing somewhat from the Near Eastern arena a new one had entered it in the shape of Germany. The successors of Bismarck did not share his view that the Balkans were not worth the bones of a Pomeranian grenadier, nor did they realise that there were to be found the causes of that Russo-German war which the old Chancellor had worked so hard to prevent. Kaiser Wilhelm II

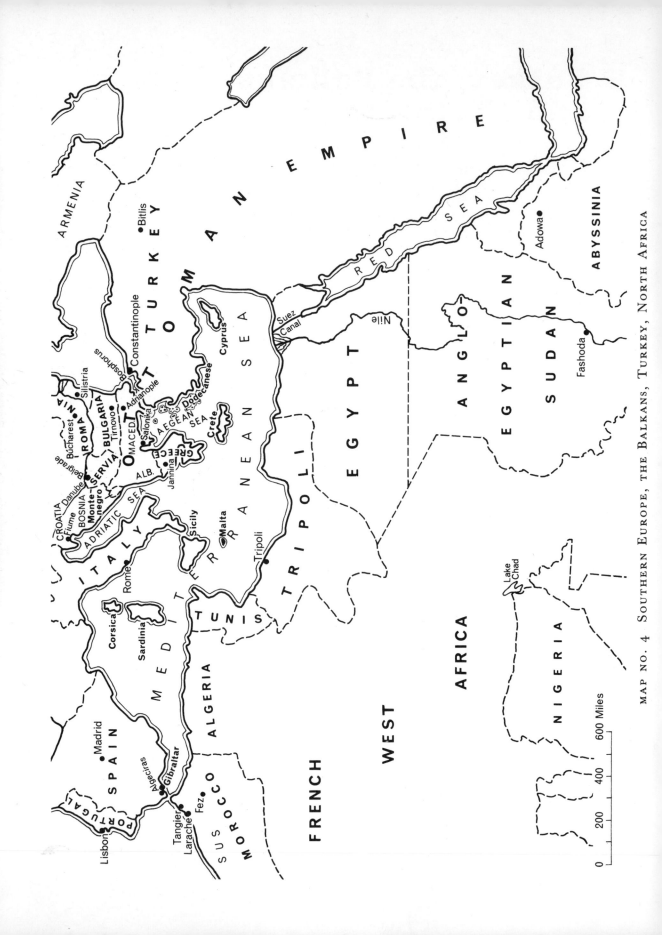

MAP NO. 4 SOUTHERN EUROPE, THE BALKANS, TURKEY, NORTH AFRICA

was determined that Germany should make her presence felt everywhere, and he was only too ready to take the place of Britain as the friend of the Turk. His intentions were first made manifest to the world at the time of the Armenian massacres, of which a brief account must be given here, for although they took place at the end of the nineteenth century their effects were felt in the early years of the twentieth.

By the Treaty of Berlin the Sultan had undertaken 'to carry out, without further delay, the ameliorations and reforms demanded in the provinces inhabited by the Armenians', but the interest which the Powers had thus taken on their behalf proved a very mixed blessing for the objects of their solicitude. The Sultan's suspicions of their loyalty were aroused, and a leading Turk observed that the best way to get rid of the Armenian problem was to get rid of the Armenians. No reforms were carried out in Armenia any more than elsewhere, and as the prospect of foreign intervention receded

44   Massacre of Armenians
in the streets of Constantinople.

Abdul Hamid II made up his mind to apply his own solution. Accordingly in 1894 there were widespread massacres in the Sasun district in the vilayet of Bitlis, which the Sultan blandly defended on the grounds that 'just as there are in other countries nihilists, socialists, and anarchists, endeavouring to obtain concessions of privileges which it is impossible to grant them, and just as steps had to be taken against them, so it is with the Armenians'.

From the beginning the British government, whether Liberal or Conservative, did all in its power to bring those responsible to justice, and to arrange for the better adminstration of Armenia in the future. In this policy London received only half-hearted support from Russia, and not even that from some of the other Powers. In these circumstances her menaces left the Sultan unaffected, for he knew that Britain stood

45 August 1903. A
detachment of Turkish
troops is cut off in the
mountains by Macedonian
rebels.

alone. At the end of September 1895 further massacres took place, and at Urfa three
thousand men, women, and children were burnt to death in the cathedral. The consular
reports left no doubt that the campaign had been carefully organised; that the slaughter
often began and ended to the call of the bugle; that regular Turkish soldiers took part
in the killing; that the authorities either instigated the tragedy or remained passive
spectators of it; and that not a single foreigner was injured. Once more the British
government tried to persuade the Concert to act, but its members contented themselves
with sending warships through the Dardanelles for the protection of their nationals.

By this time the Armenians had themselves been driven to despair, and in
August 1896 a band of the more desperate of them seized the Ottoman Bank at Galata.
The attempt to call Europe's attention to their plight by this means proved a fiasco, but
it provided the Sultan with an excuse for further repressive measures. The more fanatical
Moslems in Constantinople were armed by the government, and six to seven thousand
Armenians were killed in broad daylight in the streets of the capital. This was too much
for the Powers, who thereupon insisted that the massacre must cease, but the only
manifestation of their displeasure which Abdul Hamid was called upon to experience
was the refusal of the members of the diplomatic corps to illuminate their houses on the
occasion of his birthday a few days later.

The fact was that the Concert, with the exception of Great Britain, was not in the
least interested in the fate of the Armenians. Russia, as we have seen, was looking to
the Pacific, and was by no means desirous of reopening the Near East question.
Germany never pretended to care what became of the Christian subjects of the Sultan,

72

46   Sultan Abdul Hamid II
(1842–1918), deposed in 1909.

for whose friendship she was in any case angling, while Austria-Hungary had her own game to play. France followed her Russian ally, and Italy did not count. The United States, indeed, was far from approving of what was taking place, but Washington was not a signatory of the Treaty of Berlin, and it was still a cardinal maxim of American policy to hold aloof from European complications.

In England it was otherwise. To a generation that has known the cold-blooded extermination of six million Jews in Germany and unnumbered millions of political prisoners in the labour camps of Siberia, the Armenian massacres may seem small beer, but in the civilised atmosphere of the nineteenth century the reaction was profound. British anger was hot against Abdul Hamid, whom Gladstone denounced as 'the Great Assassin' and whom the poet William Watson cursed as 'Immortally, beyond all mortals, damned'; but in the circumstances there was nothing that the British government could do. 'Isolated action', the Liberal Rosebery declared, 'means a European war', and the Conservative Salisbury was not prepared to risk that, so Britain, though very angry, remained impotent.

The result of the Armenian crisis thus was that Germany strengthened her position at Constantinople while Britain lost further ground there, with ultimate consequences which were to be felt at the outbreak of the First World War. On a shorter term, London had been warned of her growing isolation in Europe, and this was prophetic of what was to occur three years later at the beginning of the South African War.

For a short space after these events the centre of interest in international matters was fixed elsewhere, but the twentieth century had hardly begun when Turkish misrule in Macedonia provoked another crisis. At first the Powers showed a disposition to act together, and in October 1903 the Austrian and Russian governments agreed upon what was called the Murzsteg programme of reforms, which provided for foreign officers for the *gendarmerie*, and for the division of Macedonia into zones, each administered by one of the Powers. Once more there was gone through the weary round first of applying pressure to compel the Sultan to accept the reforms in theory, and then of trying to cause him to apply them in fact. Some progress, however, had been made when in January 1908, the Austro-Hungarian government announced that it had obtained from the Porte permission to survey the route for a railway through the Sanjak of Novibazar: now this was only in accordance with the Treaty of Berlin, but projected railways were explosive material in the international politics of those days, and Russian suspicions were at once aroused, and such co-operation as there had been between St Petersburg and Vienna in the affairs of the Balkans came to an end. In July of that same year, 1908, there occurred the Young Turk Revolution, and the future of the Near East was again in the melting-pot.

The Young Turk Revolution was a seizure of power from Abdul Hamid by a group of officers, some of them neither young nor Turks, of which the most outstanding was Enver Pasha, and in retrospect we can now see that it was the prototype of that one-party government which was adopted by so many countries later in the century, while the Committee of Union and Progress had not a little in common with German National Socialism and Italian Fascism. In 1908, however, it posed as a liberal and democratic movement, and one of the first acts of Enver Pasha and his colleagues was to convoke a Parliament of the whole Ottoman Empire. This action went a long way towards rallying support for the new régime in western Europe, but it raised the question of Bosnia and Herzegovina in an acute form.

As early as 1881 the Austro-Hungarian government had reserved the right to annex the two provinces whenever it should deem the moment opportune, without encountering any serious opposition from St Petersburg, but when in 1897 Vienna proposed to reaffirm the right of annexation this provoked the cool reply from the Russian government that this would require special scrutiny at the proper time. So matters might have continued for many years but for the action of the Young Turks. Austria-Hungary was only in occupation of Bosnia and Herzegovina, for the two provinces still in theory formed part of the Ottoman Empire, and as such were entitled to send representatives to the new Turkish Parliament. Yet if this happened, and if Turkey under her new rulers really succeeded in putting her house in order, then there was considerable danger that Bosnia and Herzegovina might pass out of the keeping of Vienna altogether.

Nor was this all, for the relations between the Dual Monarchy and the Southern Slavs were becoming acute. The substitution in Belgrade in 1903 of the Russophil dynasty of Karageorgevitch for the Austrophil House of Obrenovitch meant that Vienna could no longer control her Slav subjects by means of a compliant King of Serbia, for under the new monarch, Peter I, the most chauvinistic elements in that country were already looking forward to the union of all the Southern Slavs under the Serbian Crown, and to a revival of the Serbian Empire of the Middle Ages. For more than one reason, therefore, it behoved Austria-Hungary to act before the situation got completely out of hand.

The Foreign Minister of the Dual Monarchy, Aehrenthal, realised that he could not move in the matter without Russian support, and to his surprise he found Isvolsky, his Russian counterpart, a great deal more friendly than he had supposed to be possible. The two statesmen met in Bohemia in September 1908, but as the discussion between them took place without witnesses, as nothing was committed to paper, and as the participants subsequently put out conflicting versions of what had been settled, it is not easy to be certain what exactly occurred. In the main, however, it seems to have been agreed that Austria-Hungary should be allowed to annex Bosnia and Herzegovina in return for supporting Russia's demand for the opening of the Bosphorus and the Dardanelles to Russian warships. Having, as he said, created a situation in which the

47   King Alexander and Queen Draga of Serbia. In 1903 their brutal murder caused widespread revulsion, but paved the way for a pro-Russian policy in Belgrade.

48   October 1908. King Ferdinand of Bulgaria inspects his troops. He created the Balkan League and headed a very successful army during the Balkan Wars. But after the Treaty of London, Bulgaria soon lost all she had gained.

Russian bear would growl but not bite, Aehrenthal proceeded to secure the support of Bulgaria, whose Prince Ferdinand was assured that Austria-Hungary would raise no objection if he were to proclaim his independence. Accordingly, on 5 October 1908, Bulgaria was proclaimed at Tirnovo an independent kingdom, and on the following day Franz Josef announced the annexation of Bosnia and Herzegovina to the Habsburg dominions.

75

The reaction of the Powers was an interesting commentary upon the international situation. Germany had neither suggested nor desired the annexation, and Bülow realised that it would not be too easy for him to reconcile Turkey to what had occurred: the duty and interest of the Reich to stand by his ally were, however, manifest, and the closeness of the ties which bound Vienna to Berlin was advertised by the Kaiser's appearance 'in shining armour', as he put it in a speech. Whether Bismarck would ever have allowed a situation to develop in which Germany had to follow the lead of Austria-Hungary is another matter, and it was prophetic of the course of events six years later. Clemenceau, then Prime Minister of France, was more indignant with Isvolsky for not consulting him as Russia's ally than with Aehrenthal for infringing the Treaty of Berlin, and French public opinion was not seriously alarmed. King Edward VII, on the other hand, made no secret of his annoyance, and Grey took his stand on the Berlin settlement. In these circumstances the Russian claim to compensation, which would also have constituted a violation of the Treaty of Berlin, received little support in London.

Yet if no Great Power were willing to make the annexation of the two provinces a *casus belli* the Serbs were prepared to fight. For them everything seemed to be at stake; if Bosnia and Herzegovina settled down under Habsburg rule then the very future of Serbia herself would be at stake, for the Dual Monarchy might become Triune, as it was already rumoured that the heir, the Archduke Franz Ferdinand, wished. Serbia, however, could not fight alone, and Aehrenthal's brilliant diplomacy was isolating her; Bulgaria had already been gained in advance, and the Porte was soon won over by the withdrawal of the Austrian garrisons in the Sanjak. Only Russia remained as a potential ally. Very skilfully Aehrenthal refrained from any hostile act towards Belgrade, while Germany exerted pressure on Russia. When he realised that this had been successful, for the reason that the Russian government was in no condition to fight, he announced that he was about to send an ultimatum to Belgrade. On this, as he had anticipated, the Triple Entente advised the Serbs to yield, and at the end of March 1909 Serbia recognised that her rights were not infringed by the annexation, while she undertook to cease her attitude of protest and opposition, to modify her policy towards Vienna, and to live with the Dual Monarchy on neighbourly terms.

If the Conference of Algeciras had been in some measure a drawn battle between the Triple Alliance and its opponents the Near Eastern crisis of 1908–9 had represented a triumph for what were soon to be known as the Central Powers. Austria-Hungary had gained a considerable accession of territory, and had humiliated Serbia; Germany had supported her old ally in Vienna without alienating her new friend at Constantinople; and Russia, and through her the Triple Entente, had been challenged, and had given way sooner than submit to the arbitrament of war. Such being the case it is little wonder that Bülow wrote: 'For the first time the Austro-German alliance proved its strength in a genuine conflict. The group of Powers whose influence had been so much overestimated at Algeciras fell to pieces when faced with the tough problems of continental policy.'

For the next two years there was a relaxation of international tension, though the Powers continued to pile up armaments upon an unprecedented scale, and, in particular, there was a close and ominous competition between the naval construction programme of Germany and Great Britain. In 1910 there died King Edward VII, the

49 Windsor, May 1910. The Kaiser, King George V and the
Duke of Connaught, followed by Edward Prince of Wales
(later Edward VIII; *left*) and Albert Duke of York (later
King George VI; *right*), lead the funeral procession of
Edward VII.

last British monarch to play a leading part in world politics, and during the years which
followed there was much speculation whether had his life been spared, he would have
been able to prevent or postpone the catastrophe which was so soon to overtake
Western civilisation. However this may be, the restless policy of Germany soon produced
another crisis, and thereafter, with an ever-increasing momentum, the Powers slipped
down to destruction.

The first conflict of interest was in Morocco once more. Berlin had taken full
advantage of the acceptance of its contention that the affairs of the Shereffian Empire
were the concern of the world, and German businessmen were encouraged to take part
in the development of the country. The result was more than one clash between the
various foreign firms which either had a stake in the country or were endeavouring to
secure one. This was bad enough, but in addition there was growing anarchy among the
Moors. Abdul Aziz IV was overthrown in 1908 by his brother Mulai Hafid, but the
new Sultan was hardly more secure on his throne than had been his predecessor. In
1909 the Riff tribesmen rose against Spain, who was obliged to send an army of 50,000
men to reduce them to submission. Two years later the tribes round Fez revolted, and
the capital was besieged: in his despair Mulai Hafid called upon France to save him,

50 August 1909. Spanish troops prepare to repel an attack by Riff tribesmen from the 3,000-foot high position at Mellila. In November Spain had to send in 50,000 troops to reduce the rebels.

and in accordance with his request French troops occupied Fez. The Spaniards, not to be outdone, landed a force at Larache.

German opinion, both official and public, was roused to fury by this news, and it was generally believed in the Reich that the French government was endeavouring to use the unrest in Morocco as an excuse for turning the country into another Tunis – long a French Protectorate – in violation of the Treaty of Algeciras. At the beginning of July 1911, therefore, the German government decided to challenge the French position by sending the *Panther* to Agadir, and in justification of this step Berlin announced that the Treaty of Algeciras was dead.

> Some German firms established in the South of Morocco, notably at Agadir and in the vicinity, have been alarmed by a certain ferment among the local tribes, due, it seems, to recent occurrences in other parts of the country. These firms have applied to the Imperial Government for protection of their lives and property. At their request the Government have decided to send a warship to Agadir to lend help in case of need to their subjects and *protégés* as well as to the considerable German interests in that territory. As soon as the state of affairs has resumed its normal tranquillity the ship will leave.

There is, it must be admitted, a good deal to be said for the German point of view, and the French had already been warned of the consequences of an occupation of Fez. Indeed, the repercussions of the arrival of the *Panther* at Agadir were more violent in London than in Paris, where they were followed by negotiations with the German

78

51   The German gunboat *Panther*, sent in July 1911 to
Agadir 'in order to protect German interests'; but Germany
got no political rights in Morocco.

government as to the compensation to be paid by France for a free hand in Morocco. Great Britain, on the other hand, had no desire to see Germany established on the Moroccan coast, right athwart her own lines of communication, and she was prepared to go to any lengths to prevent this. Grey denounced the voyage of the *Panther* as an unprovoked attack on the *status quo*, and Lloyd George, then Chancellor of the Exchequer, made an extremely bellicose speech at the Mansion House, when he talked of 'a peace at a price that would be a humiliation intolerable for a great country like ours to endure'.

This speech brought war very close, and three days later there were rumours – inevitable after such a speech – of orders to the British fleet. Public excitement was growing, but it subsided rapidly after a prompt denial of the rumours, and even more so after a statement by Asquith, which, though not very clear, implied that intervention at Agadir had never been in question. The British reaction had, however, made Germany realise that in the event of hostilities Britain would stand by France, so that while it inflamed German opinion it resulted in a modification of German demands. The immediate crisis passed, though there was another in the middle of August in consequence of a deadlock in the Franco-German negotiations, but the Kaiser threw his weight into the scale in favour of peace, and a settlement was reached early in November. France obtained all she wanted politically in Morocco, and in 1912 she established a Protectorate over that country; in the economic field she conceded the maintenance of tariff equality; and in return she ceded to Germany some hundred thousand square miles of the French Congo. By the end of the year British and German

79

statesmen were making friendly references to one another, and the storm seemed to have subsided as quickly as it had risen. Actually, it had left many a bitter memory and much suspicion behind it on both sides of the North Sea.

Before agreement had been reached there had been another change in the *status quo* in Africa due to the seizure of Tripoli by Italy. Her interests in that province had long been recognised by the Powers, and in September 1911 she declared war on Turkey on the somewhat inadequate pretext of ill treatment of her nationals and interference with her trade. In actual fact the Italian government was becoming fearful that when France had consolidated her position in Morocco she might cast covetous eyes on Tripoli, while an easy conquest would prove popular with public opinion at home, and would go far to erase the memory of Adowa, where the Italians had been disastrously defeated by the Abyssinians at the close of the previous century. The only serious domestic opposition came from the more extreme Socialists who looked to Mussolini, then editor of *La Lotta di Classe*, and who refused to be side-tracked from the class struggle by what he regarded as an imperialistic war; but the ease with which the conquest was effected in its earlier stages justified the hopes of Rome. The Porte had no fleet which could compare with the Italian, and although Egypt was still nominally an Ottoman province the British government refused to allow the passage of Turkish troops through that country. Italy thus had Tripoli at her mercy from the start.

Internationally the repercussions of this conflict were significant, for it marked a stage on the passage of Italy from the Triple Alliance to the Triple Entente, which was to prove of such importance when the First World War came. Certainly she did not consult the interests of her old associates. For Germany, in particular, a very difficult situation had been created by this war between two of her allies, and the Kaiser was not a little annoyed at this disturbance of German plans to win the support of Moslem opinion. The Triple Entente, on the other hand, made no protest against the action of Italy, though in Great Britain at any rate there was general reprobation at this sudden and unprovoked attack. The government, however, was too wise to let its heart run away with its head, and Grey knew that any attempt at interference would merely drive Italy back into the arms of Germany without being of the least assistance to the Turks.

52   Italian troops on the march in North Africa during their Tripoli campaign, which caused embarrassment among the Powers. It took the Italians until August 1914 to master the interior, in face of bitter Arab and Berber opposition.

At the same time the Powers insisted that the actual fighting should be confined within certain limits. Italy was allowed to capture the Dodecanese but Austria-Hungary placed her veto upon any attack on European Turkey, and the Italians were not permitted to blockade the Dardanelles. In these circumstances the war dragged on for some time, and, as we shall see, it might have continued even longer but for the foundation of the Balkan League: the Turks were desirous of getting rid of the old enemy in view of the advent of a new one, and Italy did not wish to be placed on the same footing as the Balkan States. Peace was accordingly made at Ouchy in October 1912; Turkey ceded Tripoli to Italy, who was in her turn to restore the Dodecanese to the Porte; this last provision was, however, never carried out, for, realising that they were quite unable to protect the islands from seizure by the Greeks, the Turks were quite willing for them to remain in Italian hands, which they were to do for many years.

The events which caused the Porte to come to terms with Italy were the formation of the Balkan League and its victories in the field. The author of this alliance was the Bulgarian Prime Minister, Gueshoff, for he and his master, King Ferdinand, had come to the conclusion that the aspirations of Bulgaria could only be satisfied in co-operation with the other Balkan States, and on this account they were prepared to sink, for the time being, their differences with Serbia. With the full support of Russia, once more actively interested in the affairs of South-East Europe, a treaty between Serbia and Bulgaria was signed in March 1912; in May the Greek government joined the alliance, a military convention following in September; and in August the adhesion of Montenegro was secured. Ostensibly these documents provided for mutual support if one of the Great Powers tried to annex or occupy any Balkan territory under Turkish rule, but there was a secret annex which provided for common action by the larger States, subject to the approval of Russia, against the Porte in the event of disturbance or menaces of war in the Ottoman Empire. The Russian government, it may be added, by no means kept its French ally fully informed of what was afoot, and Poincaré, then Prime Minister, was far from pleased when he came to learn the truth.

As the summer began to pass into autumn the tension increased; Turkish promises of reform in Albania evoked complaints of neglect from Sofia and Belgrade, and Montenegro commenced to mobilise. With the advent of October the progress of events was accelerated. The Powers had for weeks been trying to agree upon a common plan of action, and on 7 October, Austria-Hungary and Russia were authorised to inform the Balkan States that the Concert condemned any steps likely to cause a breach with the Porte, that it would itself take the enforcement of the reforms in hand, and that no change in the *status quo*, as a result of war, would be allowed. This declaration came too late, for on 8 October Montenegro took up arms, and the other Christian States immediately followed her example. Contrary to general expectation the Turks proved no match for their foes, and on 3 November, with the Bulgarians threatening Constantinople itself, the Porte asked for the intervention of the Powers.

The sweeping victories of the Balkan States were by no means to the liking of the Triple Alliance. Germany saw her Turkish ally weakened, and Russian policy triumphant, while Austria-Hungary and Italy were firmly opposed to the acquisition by Serbia of a port on the Adriatic. On the other side, Great Britain and France were more concerned with preventing an extension of the struggle than with any other aspect of the situation, and from December 1912 to March of the following year the danger of war between Russia and Austria-Hungary was acute. There were, however, strong moderating influences at work, and the Kaiser told the Imperial Chancellor, Bethmann-Hollweg, that he would not march on Paris or Warsaw for the sake of Albania, while Franz Josef refused to listen to the counsels of the extremists in Vienna and Budapest, and he was strengthened in this attitude by the notification from Berlin that Austria-Hungary would only receive German support if she were herself actually the victim of aggression.

In these circumstances a conference of the ambassadors of the Powers was called into being in London, where it sat from December 1912 onwards under the chairman-ship of the British Foreign Secretary, Sir Edward Grey, but before Vienna would consent to take part in it an assurance was given that the permanent establishment of Serbia on the Adriatic would be excluded from discussion. It may be added that throughout the conference Great Britain and Germany worked in perfect accord.

Meanwhile, the situation in the Balkan Peninsula itself was marked by the most violent changes of fortune. The representatives of the belligerents signed a treaty in London in December 1912, but it was promptly repudiated by Enver Pasha in Constantinople. When fighting was renewed Adrianople fell to the combined attack of the Bulgarians and Serbs, and the Greeks captured Jannina. At the end of May 1913, therefore, the Porte was compelled to sign a treaty by which Greece obtained Salonika, southern Macedonia, and Crete; Serbia secured control of northern Macedonia; and to Bulgaria was assigned Thrace and the Aegean coast, though she had to surrender Silistria to Romania, for no particular reason. As for Turkey, she emerged from the settlement with nothing but Constantinople and a foothold in eastern Thrace.

A month had hardly elapsed after the conclusion of this agreement before the Bulgarians fell on the Serbian forces in Macedonia, while another Bulgarian army made a dash for Salonika. Once more the Balkans appeared to be in the melting-pot, but it

53   King Nicholas of Montenegro (1841–1921), with some of his elderly reserve troops. Despot, fighter and poet, he was the first to declare war on Turkey to begin the Balkan Wars. He won territory, but faced agitation for union with Serbia.

54　A commissariat train of the Greek army. The Greek armies enjoyed tremendous success during the first Balkan War.

55　November 1912. King George I of Greece rides through the streets of Salonika after the Greek capture of the city. On 18 March 1913 he was assassinated there.

soon transpired that King Ferdinand had taken on a task which was beyond his country's strength. The Serbs and Greeks withstood the Bulgarian onslaught, while the Romanian government, determined to prevent a Bulgarian hegemony, sent an army across the Danube; even the Turks plucked up enough courage to recapture Adrianople. The result was the Treaty of Bucharest in August 1913, by which Bulgaria lost not only her access to the Aegean and her gains in Macedonia, but was also compelled to cede to Romania territory with a population of 340,000. The Turks retained Adrianople. All that now remained was for the Powers to create that independent Albania which was the logical outcome of the refusal to allow Serbia an outlet to the Adriatic: by the end of the year 1913 this task had been accomplished, and the Balkans were, in theory at any rate, once more at peace.

The crisis had proved that a general war could be averted by co-operation between Great Britain and Germany, and by that alone: Russia and Austria-Hungary had partially mobilised in 1912, and had only been held back with the greatest difficulty. Yet in Germany the strength of militarism was growing, and the Kaiser was coming to believe that war with France was inevitable. 'The whole of Germany is charged with electricity', the American Colonel House reported after a visit to Berlin in May 1913. Everybody's nerves were tense. It only required a spark to set the whole thing off. In Paris the feeling was much the same, and a series of Franco-German incidents served to fan the flame of French chauvinism. From Vienna the French Ambassador was reporting that 'the feeling that the nations are moving towards a conflict, urged by an irresistible force, grows from day to day', while at the beginning of 1914 the Tsar said, 'For Serbia we will do everything.' No single statesman could, in these circumstances, prevent the breaking of the storm, but so long as the British and the Germans refused to allow their hands to be forced there was a hope that war might be postponed. As late as June 1914 an agreement was reached between London and Berlin regarding the vexed question of the Baghdad Railway by which Britain secured her position in the Persian Gulf while recognising the whole of Mesopotamia north of Basra as within the German sphere of influence.

83

6 The Development of the U.S.A.

THE BASIC FACT of American history is that the United States charged headlong in a hundred and fifty years through the whole cycle from primitive agriculture to cosmopolitanism; and she has never known a time of rest, or of calm self-possession. As one of her leading historians has written, 'America had done everything by 1900, except compose her soul; an act which she omitted by necessity, not by choice.' At the beginning of the nineteenth century Jefferson gave the United States a thousand years to reach the Mississippi, whereas in fact she got to the Pacific in fifty.

New towns and industries sprang up with unprecedented rapidity, and this was followed by a change in the volume and source of immigration, which in its turn brought about a social revolution. For this there were three main reasons. Firstly, the mines and factories, growing by geometrical progression, were searching desperately for cheap labour. Secondly, the transcontinental railways needed customers for their enormous holdings of land, because unless the population increased with quite abnormal speed many of them would go bankrupt. Thirdly, the steamship companies were eager for steerage passengers, and their advertisements, appealing to the poorer and more oppressed peoples of Europe, reinforced those of the railways: according to evidence given before the Immigration Commission two of the steamship lines had between five and six thousand ticket agents in the year 1911 in Galicia alone.

As a result of these forces, as well as of the overpopulation and racial intolerance in some parts of southern and eastern Europe, not only the number but the nature of the citizens of the United States was suddenly changed. The figures are impressive. In the decade before the Civil War she received two and a half million immigrants; in the decade 1871 to 1880 the figure had hardly risen; but in the next ten years it was five and a quarter millions. Then came a drop because of the long depression of the nineties, but between 1901 and 1910 almost nine million immigrants entered the United States, and between 1911 and 1920 almost six million. Even more interesting than the rise in numbers was the change in the country of origin. Until 1880 the large majority of immigrants came from northern and western Europe, so that the American racial stock remained predominantly English, Irish, Scottish, German, and Scandinavian, but the change came with the rise of the cities and of the new industries: during the twenty years from 1891 to 1910 twelve and a half million foreigners settled in the United States, and more than eight million of them constituted the so-called 'new immigration' from Italy, Poland, Hungary, Bohemia, Slovakia, Croatia, and Greece. The total population rose from 76,000,000 in 1900 to 92,000,000 in 1910, and 106,000,000 in 1920.

Most of the 'old immigration' from northern Europe now moved West and took up land, though many Germans settled in the towns in the Middle West. The Irish were the exception, for they tended to stay in the East, and to earn their living by unskilled labour and by politics: from the former occupation, though not from the latter, they were soon ousted by the new immigrants, who were for the most part manual workers, and who were in any event too poor to buy farms or farm equipment. In these circum-

56   New York, 1892. Russian Jewish refugees land from
their tender at the Barge Office. The United States was a
promised land after the pogroms of eastern Europe.

stances they quickly sank to the bottom of the labour market, and were to be found in
mines, factories, railway-construction camps, and lumber camps. Since they were
separated from the native Americans by language, customs, and religion they tended to
stay together in colonies in the big cities: they had come from the land, and most of
them had seen enough of it, preferring even the worst urban slums. The one region
where the new immigrants did not encroach upon the lowest-paid jobs was the South,
and there the Negro maintained his melancholy right to the harshest forms of labour,
the only exception being the Mexicans who streamed into Texas, New Mexico, and
Arizona, and the Cuban and Puerto Rican cigar-makers who settled in Florida.

During the first hundred years of independence the federal government left the
control of immigration almost wholly to the states at whose ports the immigrants
landed, but in 1882 Congress prohibited Chinese from entering the country, at first for
a period of ten years, but later the exclusion was made permanent. President Theodore
Roosevelt sought to control Japanese immigration without reverting to such drastic
methods, but by means of a 'gentleman's agreement' between the two governments:
this, however, did not go far enough to please the Pacific States, though it was not until
after the First World War that the Japanese were kept out by law. To European
immigrants the principle of selection had been applied in the eighties, but it was not
until after 1918 that the present quota system came into full force.

The outstanding figure in the United States in the opening years of the twentieth
century was Theodore Roosevelt, to whom allusion has already been made. He had

85

been born in New York in 1858, and his father was descended from one of the early Dutch settlers in what was then New Amsterdam, while his mother was a Southerner from Georgia, with Scottish-Irish and Huguenot blood. As a child he was delicate, but he set his mind on growing strong, and by the time that he went to Harvard he had repaired most of his bodily weaknesses, except the defective eyesight which was to trouble him throughout life. Politics early attracted him, and he entered the New York State legislature, which was in those days an unconventional step for a well-to-do youth of good family. His friends warned him that his associates would be 'grooms, liquor dealers, and low politicians'. 'In that case', he answered, 'they belong to the governing class, and you do not. I mean, if I can, to be one of the governing class.' Roosevelt was a strong Republican, and he could not help feeling that God intended Republicans to be better than Democrats. He was also an exceedingly hard worker, and his friend William Allen White wrote of him, 'The thing which the gods gave Roosevelt in excess was energy. He was Gargantuan in his capacity for work.' He was also an extrovert of no mean proportions.

Then, in the eighties, he abandoned politics altogether for five years, and bought two cattle ranches in what was at that time the Dakota Territory. It is true that he lost in the venture some fifty thousand dollars which he could ill afford, but he gained a knowledge of the West that was to be of the greatest value to him, and he was the first President to know the Great Plains from personal experience. Further evidence of Roosevelt's versatility is the fact that by the time he returned to political life he had published seven books, including *The Naval War of 1812* and *Gouverneur Morris*. When he settled in Washington he and his wife went about in society a good deal, especially in the set of which the outstanding figures were John Hay and Henry Adams, together with the Cabot Lodges and Cecil Spring Rice of the British Embassy.

When the Republicans came into power with the election of Benjamin Harrison to the Presidency in 1888, Roosevelt was appointed a Civil Service Commissioner, an

57 A busy street in Chicago, already a great commercial centre, famous for its contributions in the history of organised labour and civic reform.

86

office which had not amounted to much in the past: now, however, it became a great scene of activity and publicity, and Roosevelt managed to get twenty thousand federal employees transferred from the spoils system to the civil service. His next appointment was, back in his native New York, as President of the Board of Police Commissioners, and here again he soon saw to it that he was always in the centre of the stage. As Mr Herbert Agar has well put it, 'Every strife in which Roosevelt engaged became to him a battle in a glorious war between right and wrong. If he dismissed a thieving policeman, he somehow made it sound like a chapter in *Pilgrim's Progress*.' In the political world such antics rarely commend a man to the leaders of his party, and Roosevelt was no exception, so many strings had to be pulled by his friends before he was offered the post of Assistant Secretary to the Navy.

The outbreak of war between Spain and the United States in 1898 gave Roosevelt the opportunity to become a national figure, and he was quick to take advantage of it. He left Washington to raise a regiment of volunteer cavalry, called the 'Rough Riders', and they were an odd collection of cowboys, ranchers, college athletes, and New York policemen. Soon they and their Colonel were front-page news, and when the war finished Roosevelt was a hero from coast to coast. He was promptly elected Governor of New York, and then Vice-President of the United States, though President McKinley was by no means desirous of having him as his colleague. 'Don't any of you realise', said the Conservative Hanna, 'that there's only one life between this madman and the White House?', but the general belief in the Republican hierarchy was that he had been buried in the Vice-Presidency, and would cause no more trouble by his unorthodox views: then the unexpected happened, McKinley was murdered, and on 14 September 1901 the 'madman' became President.

During his seven years in office Roosevelt came to believe firmly in more power for the central government as compared with the states, in more power for the President as compared with Congress, and in less power for Wall Street as compared with

58 Boston, Massachusetts. By the early twentieth century Boston had lost its English influence and was now predominantly Irish with inflows of Jewish, Italian, Polish and Scandinavian immigrants.

87

59 Negroes weighing the crop on a cotton plantation in
Georgia. In this state the Negro was virtually disfranchised
in 1900 by 'grandfather' laws which required a registrant to
be a 'veteran of any war' or 'the descendant of a veteran'.

Washington. He explained his views on this last point in 1905. 'The great development
of industrialism', he said, 'says that there must be an increase in the supervision
exercised by the Government over business enterprise.' Government, in his view, must
make sure that the power of wealth is 'used for and not against the interests of the
people as a whole. . . . We do not intend that the Republic shall ever fail as those
Republics of olden times failed, in which there finally came to be a government by
classes, which resulted either in the poor plundering the rich or in the rich . . . exploiting
the poor.' With the arrival of Theodore Roosevelt at the White House a new era in
American politics began: the men of the Civil War were gone for ever.

Late in his second term Roosevelt's relations with Congress became unhappy,
probably because he had a view of the powers of the Presidency which no Congress
could accept. 'I have a definite philosophy about the Presidency,' he wrote to an
English historian, 'I think it should be a very powerful office, and I think the President
should be a very strong man who uses without hesitation every power that the position
yields', while in his *Autobiography* he boasted, 'I did not usurp power, but I did greatly
broaden the use of executive power.' No President with such views could expect a long
peace with Congress.

Meanwhile, as early as 1902, Roosevelt had begun to act against the trusts, which
may best be defined as a combination of business entities formed to reduce competition.
In February of that year Attorney-General Philander Knox announced that the government would ask the dissolution of the Northern Security Company on the ground that
it transgressed the Sherman Act, which was aimed at restraining the activities of trusts
but had not been put into force during McKinley's Presidency. Those trusts were hated

60 J. Pierpoint Morgan (1837–1913), the American financier and art and book collector, and philanthropist. He left some $70 million.

by the Trade Unions on account of their size and impersonality; by small businessmen for their piratical methods; by economic theorists for their tendency to destroy the system of competition and enterprise; and by consumers who had to accept monopoly prices. Naturally those who operated the trusts took a different view, and one of them was J. Pierpoint Morgan, who, when he heard that proceedings were pending against one of his companies, hurried to Washington. 'If we have done anything wrong,' he said to the President, 'send your man [meaning the Attorney-General] to my man [meaning one of his lawyers] and they can fix it up.' To which Knox answered, 'We don't want to fix it up; we want to stop it.' Then Morgan asked whether the President meant to 'attack any other interests'. 'Certainly not', said Roosevelt, 'unless we find out . . . they have done something we regard as wrong.' After Morgan had left, Roosevelt said to Knox, 'That is a most illuminating illustration of the Wall Street point of view. Mr. Morgan could not help regarding me as a big rival speculator, who either intended to ruin all his interests or else be induced to come to an agreement to ruin none.' He expressed his views quite forcibly when in a letter to King Edward VII he said, 'With us it is not as it is with you; our men of vast wealth do not fully realise that great responsibility must always go hand in hand with great privilege.'

Roosevelt certainly made the Sherman Act effective. Before he left the White House he had started twenty-five proceedings which led to indictments; his successor, Taft, began forty-five; while in 1914 Woodrow Wilson went even further and secured the passage of the Clayton Act and the Federal Trade Commission Act, which greatly strengthened the government in its fight against monopoly. The Clayton Act forbade practices which substantially tended to lessen competition, such as discrimination in prices, the acquisition of stock in one company by another, and interlocking directorates. It also prohibited the use of injunctions 'unless necessary to prevent irreparable injury to property, or to a property right . . . for which injury there is no adequate remedy at law'. At the same time the Federal Trade Commission was set up to investigate businesses engaged in inter-state commerce, to determine whether there had been violations of the anti-trust laws, and when necessary to issue orders to 'cease and desist'.

In one field Roosevelt had a much freer hand, and that was foreign affairs. Some of his actions would, it is true, hardly commend themselves to the moral sense of today, but it was an age of Imperialism, and the President was very definitely an Imperialist. Among other things the recent struggle with Spain had underlined the need for easier communication between the East and West coasts of the United States, in other words it had given a new importance to the project for an inter-oceanic canal. Such a canal had been discussed for many years, and as early as 1850 the United States and Great Britain had signed a treaty providing for the joint control of such a waterway. The United States had, however, become increasingly restive at the delay in carrying out this bargain, and in 1900 the British government, alarmed at its proved isolation during the South African War, was anxious for American friendship, and in the Hay-Pauncefote Treaty conceded exclusive rights to the United States. The Senate approved the treaty within a month.

So far, so good, but it now remained to settle with Colombia, through whose province of Panama the canal was to pass. A treaty was drafted, but was rejected by the Colombian Congress, and the situation was not improved when Roosevelt referred to its members as 'inefficient bandits'. The situation was further complicated by the existence of a French company which had rights in the canal, which Washington proposed to buy for a fair sum, and by a section of opinion in Panama which stood to gain by the construction of the waterway. In November 1903 after a little judicious prodding by the company's representatives Panama underwent what Roosevelt called 'a most just and proper revolution'. American warships were in the neighbourhood; American marines were landed; and the Colombian troops on the spot were persuaded to renounce any attempt to suppress the revolt. The new State of Panama was recognised an hour and sixteen minutes after it was born, and eleven days later its government signed the treaty which Bogotá had refused. To give it its due, Congress was none too happy about this gunboat diplomacy, but the President did not care. 'I took the canal zone', he later remarked, 'and let Congress debate, and while the debate goes on the canal does also.'

There were other respects in which the Roosevelt period was one of expanding American influence over the countries of the Caribbean. The United States withdrew

61 4 March 1905. Theodore Roosevelt (1858–1919) delivers his inaugural address in front of the Capitol, Washington, after being elected to the Presidency by popular vote.

90

62　December 1902. Ships of the British North American squadron blockade the Venezuelan coast. In the centre is the flagship *Ariadne*. The U.S.A. forced arbitration in the dispute between Britain and Germany, and Venezuela.

from Cuba in 1902, but only after compelling the Cuban government to agree, in what became known as the Platt Amendment, to an American right of intervention 'for the purpose of preserving order and maintaining Cuban independence', to the acquisition of a naval base in the island, and to a promise not to incur too large an indebtedness. American troops were in the island again in 1906, and remained there until 1909, though it is only fair to say that in this case the administration acted most reluctantly.

More important was the new twist that Roosevelt gave to the Monroe Doctrine. American opinion had been roused in 1902 when Great Britain and Germany sent a naval force to blockade the Venezuelan coast as a means of bringing pressure to bear upon a dictator of the name of Cipriano Castro, but the incident passed off without any international explosion. At the same time Roosevelt, being the man he was, began to think about the danger contingent upon European intervention ostensibly for the vindication of just claims, but in some cases directed towards occupation of territory in the Americas. Such occupation could be dangerous, especially in the Caribbean. Accordingly, not without the support of Great Britain, who was, as has been shown, beginning to limit her commitments in the New World, Roosevelt in 1904 laid down a new principle, namely that 'chronic wrong-doing may in America, as elsewhere, ultimately require intervention by some civilised nation, and in the Western hemisphere the adherence of the United States to the Monroe Doctrine may force the United States, however reluctantly, in flagrant cases of wrong-doing or importance to the exercise of an international police power'. In effect, the United States was in future to be the policeman of the New World.

A test case occurred in that very same year when the Dominican Republic was threatened with intervention from Europe. 'If we are willing', said the President, 'to let Germany or England act as the policeman of the Caribbean, then we can afford not to interfere when gross wrong-doing occurs, but if we intend to say "hands off" to the Powers of Europe, sooner or later we must keep order ourselves', so with a little pressure from Washington the Dominican government invited the President to set up a financial receivership, with an American to collect and spend the revenues of their Republic. In other fields, we have already seen the part Roosevelt played in the Moroccan crisis of 1906, and during his Presidency the American fleet did its first world cruise.

The victory over Spain marked the definite and final emergence of the United States as a potential World Power, whether its citizens liked it or not, and many of them, possibly even the large majority, did not like it at all. Of this tendency Theodore Roosevelt was the embodiment. Time and time again his successors and his fellow countrymen tried to get back to the shelter of isolation, but they found there was no return along that path, and on each occasion a large number of them came to realise that they must shoulder the responsibilities which they could no longer escape. The conquest of the Philippines brought the United States into very much closer contact with the problems of the Far East, and it was no mere coincidence that two years later its forces formed part of the international army which marched to Pekin at the time of the Boxer Rising; indeed, the first step had been taken along the road which led to Pearl Harbor. Equally, the acquisition of Cuba, temporary though this proved to be, involved Washington more deeply than ever before in the affairs of Latin America, and this had consequences which were not always too happy.

One result of the emergence of the United States from her previous isolation was, strangely enough, a steady improvement in relations between London and Washington. It would seem that the acquisition of Imperial responsibilities did much to make Americans understand the difficulties of the British; however this may be, the beginning of the twentieth century marked the growth of a friendship which was one day to develop into co-operation on the battlefield. In 1908 Roosevelt wrote to King Edward VII, 'I feel very strongly that the real interests of the English-speaking peoples are one, alike in the Atlantic and Pacific.' This was in marked contrast with what had gone before, for there had been many acrimonious disputes between Great Britain and the United States. The two countries disagreed on such questions as the boundary of Venezuela, the Bering Sea problem, fishing rights in waters off Canada, and the control over the Panama Canal. The Venezuela dispute of 1895, unlike that seven years later, very nearly led to war, but resort was finally had to arbitration, and with the turn of the century an entirely different spirit began to prevail between the two countries.

When Theodore Roosevelt left the White House in 1909 he was succeeded by another Republican in the person of William Taft, who had been Secretary of War in his predecessor's administration, and was his predecessor's choice. The new President was genial, intelligent, unassertive, and rotund; he was a good lawyer, and an experienced administrator; but he was quite unskilled as a politician. The result was that within a short time the Republicans had not only lost control of the House of Representatives but had begun to quarrel among themselves, giving the Democrats an excuse for describing them as the party of mere wealth. 'Taft', said Senator Dolliver of Iowa, 'is an amiable island entirely surrounded by men who know exactly what they want.'

His worst blunder of all was in connection with the proposed reciprocity treaty with Canada in the matter of natural products. The Progressive Republicans from the grain-growing states accused him of selling the farmers to the trusts, for they declared that Canadian food would destroy the home market while American manufacturers moved profitably into Canada, but, all the same, the President managed to push his proposal through Congress. On the Canadian side there was widespread fear that reciprocity would prove to be the first step towards annexation, and this apprehension was certainly not allayed by the indiscreet remarks of prominent Americans, including Taft himself, who declared that 'the amount of Canadian products that we would take would make Canada only an adjunct of the United States. It would transfer all their important business to Chicago and New York, with their bank credits and everything else; and it would increase greatly the demand of Canada for our manufactures.' Possibly this was true, but it was at the moment an impolitic statement to make in regard to American relations with a proud and sensitive neighbour. In the circumstances it is hardly surprising that the Canadian electorate rejected the government which advocated the treaty, and reciprocity with it.

By this time the Republican Party was in complete disarray, for as a result of the President's ineptitude the National Republican Progressive League was formed in January 1911 at Senator La Follette's house in Washington, and the Senator was put forward as the Progressive candidate for the Republican presidential nomination. The split within the party was thus made official.

At this point a new force appeared upon the scene in the person of Theodore Roosevelt, who had spent the time since his departure from the White House in attending the funeral of King Edward VII, in hunting game in Africa, and in making speeches in Europe. Shortly after his return from Europe the ex-President had said, 'I stand for the square deal. . . . I stand not merely for fair play under the present rules of the game, but I stand for having those rules changed so as to work for a more substantial equality of opportunity and of reward for equally good service.' This was little short of red revolution to Senator Aldrich and the 'Standpatters', and if he had not appreciated the fact before Roosevelt soon came to realise that when he handed the Republican Party leadership to Taft he had in fact handed it to the 'Standpatters'. It has been suggested that the realisation of this fact did not improve his temper at the time.

However this may be, and in spite of repeated pronouncements that he had finished with politics, Roosevelt was soon back in the fray. In February 1912 he arranged to receive an open letter from seven Republican governors asking him to become a candidate for the presidential nomination, and La Follette's supporters rallied to him. Before the end of the month Roosevelt announced his candidature, and in the thirteen states which chose delegates to the Convention at primary elections he won 278 delegates as against Taft's 46. This looked promising, but the President could count on the party bosses and the local machines, and they controlled the Convention, its Chairman, and its major committees. They were certainly not prepared to go down

63   A tugboat successfully passes the flight of locks leading to the Gatun Lake, before the opening ceremony of the Panama Canal in 1913.

64 President-elect Woodrow Wilson (1856–1924) and
President Taft (1857–1930) on their way to the former's
inauguration in March 1913. Taft later became Professor of
Law at Yale and in 1921 Chief Justice.

without a fight, and seeing that Taft was sure to be nominated Roosevelt and his
followers seceded from the Convention; they formed the Progressive Party, which at
its own 'Bull Moose' Convention at once nominated Roosevelt for the Presidency.

That was in August 1912 and there was not time for the Progressives to build up
an effective machine before the election was on them. The split between Roosevelt and
Taft let the Democrats in, and the figures were:

Wilson   6,286,214   Roosevelt   4,126,020   Taft   3,483,922

Taft only carried two states, Vermont and Utah, and Roosevelt five – Michigan,
Minnesota, Pennsylvania, South Dakota, and Washington, while one, namely Cali-
fornia, was divided, giving eleven electors to Roosevelt and two to Wilson. In the
electoral college Wilson had 435 votes, Roosevelt 88, and Taft a mere 8.

This election proved to be the end of Theodore Roosevelt's remarkable political
career, and it is difficult to resist the conclusion that he was himself largely responsible
for his own misfortune. The conservative wing of the Republican Party did indeed
control the machine, but only because he had handed it to them by mistake when he
supported Taft in 1908: even so, had he not split the party with his 'Bull Moose' antics
he would in all probability have regained control of it by 1916 when Wilson only just
scraped home: in 1919 he died.

If Taft was one of the most mediocre men to reach the White House his successor,
Woodrow Wilson, was to prove one of the most exceptional. He had been born in 1856
in Virginia, while his paternal grandfather came from Ulster, and his maternal one
from Glasgow, so he was predominantly what is known as 'Scotch-Irish', a mixture
which has played a great part in the history of the United States: his father was a
Presbyterian minister. Wilson spent the early and formative years of his life in Georgia
and South Carolina, so that he saw at first hand something of reconstruction in the
South after the Civil War. In 1879 he graduated from Princeton University; he then

graduated in law at the University of Virginia; and for a time taught history and political economy at Bryn Mawr College. In 1890 he returned to Princeton as Professor of Jurisprudence and Political Economy, and twelve years later he became President of the University. In this capacity he was soon engaged in his first big struggle, for Princeton had of late become a preserve of the rich, and when Wilson set out to end this monopoly he soon found himself in opposition to many of the faculty, to some of the student body, and to the wealthier *Alumni*.

The line that he took in the university called attention to qualities in him which had been unsuspected, and the Democratic Party in New Jersey began to wonder if Wilson might not be the man to carry their banner to victory in the contest for the Governorship. The politics of the state were in a peculiarly unsavoury condition, for the bosses of the two parties were in secret alliance, and they exchanged the more valuable offices, dividing spoils and patronage as they chose. This long corruption at length bred a revolt, and as a result Wilson was elected Governor by a majority of nearly fifty thousand. Once in office he defied all the political bosses, and pushed through the state legislature a number of reforms such as a Direct Primaries Act, a Corrupt Practices Act, and an Employers' Liability Act, while he created a public utilities commission to curb the corporations; furthermore, after a sharp fight he got through what were known as the 'Seven Sisters', that is to say a series of bills designed to protect the public from exploitation by the trusts. With such a record it is hardly surprising that the Democratic Party, seeking to profit by the Republican split between Roosevelt and Taft, should have turned to Wilson as a likely candidate for the Presidency, though he was only finally nominated on the forty-sixth ballot.

In character Wilson recalled Jefferson more than any other of his predecessors at the White House, though he did not go so far as never to appear in public, and to deal even with his family by letter. 'High-minded and cold-blooded', was the description of him by one member of his Cabinet, and a prominent journalist called him 'a cold fish', adding that 'the hand he gave me to shake felt like a ten-cent pickled mackerel in brown paper – irresponsive and lifeless'. Wilson's conception of his position as President was clear and uncompromising. He firmly believed that a modern State could only discharge its immense and increasing responsibilities with strong leadership, and he had no doubt whatever that the American Constitution allowed the President to take any power that was needed. He was determined to be himself a very strong head of the executive, and to be the master of the government. During the years which lay ahead his success and his failure were both to be beyond precedent.

Only a little more than twelve months were to elapse before the outbreak of the First World War, but in this halcyon period Wilson received everything that he asked from Congress, usually on his own terms. One of his earliest actions was to prove that he meant what he said about leadership by delivering his messages in person before the two houses of Congress, which had not been done since the days of John Adams, and he spent hours in his room in the Capitol pressing for action on the Bills which his administration had introduced; when all else failed he would appeal to the public over the head of Congress – a procedure which was to land him in serious trouble when he applied it to European problems after the war.

His legislation covered a wide field, and among the more prominent measures was the Underwood Tariff Bill which reduced the average duty to about 27 per cent, greatly

95

increased the free list, and provided for a tax on incomes of three thousand dollars and over. Equally important was the Federal Reserve Act which divided the country into twelve districts each with a Federal Reserve Bank, but although this system was an improvement wherever it prevailed there were still too many small banks which failed with monotonous regularity. Another great Act was the Clayton Anti-Trust Act, to which reference has already been made, which gave organised labour its charter of freedom by providing that labour unions should not be considered unlawful combinations, and that strikes, boycotts, and picketing were not as such violations of the law. In effect, during this short period no administration in American history could point to finer accomplishments in the domestic sphere.

The Wilson administration had also much to show to its credit where the Philippines were concerned. The honeymoon between the Americans and Filipinos on the morrow of the expulsion of the Spaniards had not been of long continuance, and they were soon at blows. From then the situation went from bad to worse: the American had beaten the Filipino, and meant that never for one moment should he forget it, as he soon came to realise that in getting rid of the Spaniards he had merely exchanged masters. At this point Taft was sent out to operate a more conciliatory policy, but he met with the determined opposition of the local Americans who sang of the Filipino, 'He may be a brother of William H. Taft, but he ain't no brother of mine'. Taft undoubtedly effected a great deal both at Manila and later as President, but he made the mistake of believing that the Filipinos could be won over to complete acquiescence in American domination, and that they would be so well satisfied with the bland and generous treatment he accorded them that all national aspirations would gradually disappear. It was the policy which the English were ineffectually trying to put in Ireland.

Woodrow Wilson was subject to no such illusions, and in any event it was his policy to grant self-government to the Filipinos, and to hasten the day of their independence. With this end in view he sent out as Governor-General Francis Burton Harrison in October 1913.

65　The United States battleship *Mississippi*, with a small plane embarked, steams towards Vera Cruz in April 1914.

In the field of foreign affairs it was another story. Roosevelt had entered into commitments with the Latin American Republics in which his successors became even more deeply involved. The first instance was the Dominican Republic, whose politics were very troubled, and which had a number of European creditors. In order to keep it out of further trouble Roosevelt engineered an arrangement by which the Dominican Customs houses were brought under American control; the Senate, however, refused to agree to this, so the President sent men-of-war to the coast of the Republic to prevent any new revolutionary outbreaks, and carried out his policy by means of a new understanding between the American and Dominican administrations. This worked for a time, but under Taft and Wilson armed interference did actually take place.

Secretary Knox, Taft's Secretary of State, entered into a somewhat similar arrangement with Nicaragua, but in this case matters soon reached a crisis. The régime with which the treaty was negotiated was threatened with revolution; advances had been made to it by American bankers at the request of the State Department; and in order to protect its position with regard to these same bankers the administration found it necessary to intervene. It would, however, be unfair to say that the White House acted under pressure from Big Business. The trouble was that for years diplomatic and consular offices in the Latin American countries had too often been filled by utterly unworthy men, and the appointments used as petty political rewards or dictated by selfish business interests. If the United States really wished to deserve the respect of its southern neighbours and to convince them of its good intentions, the men sent to represent her should have been of the highest calibre. As a matter of fact both Democratic and Republican administrations had for years often, though not always, sent men who, if not actually corrupt, were unfitted for such positions. There was, of course, some excuse for poor appointments. Many of the posts were more or less undesirable. They were located in sometimes unhealthy tropical capitals, with low salaries, and, since the appointees were not 'career men', there was little prospect of advancement.

Wilson's chief commitment was Mexico. For many years American relations with this southern neighbour had been excellent. There were large investments in the country amounting to something like a billion dollars, and controlling it was Porfirio Diaz who was quite content to act as the handy-man of capitalism. Unfortunately, he was sitting on a volcano, and when this erupted trouble began: Diaz was overthrown, and in the unsettled conditions of 1911 and 1912 there began a clamour for intervention. Taft, however, took no action beyond reinforcing the troops along the frontier, so the responsibility for dealing with a rapidly deteriorating situation fell on Wilson.

At this point the situation became further complicated by personal considerations. Francisco Madero was not a strong President, and he was deposed by a *coup d'état* which replaced him by Victoriano Huerta: the next step was Madero's murder, probably at the instigation of Huerta. Wilson was horrified at these events, and declared that he would not recognise a government that had attained power by violence: he seems, indeed, to have developed a personal dislike of Huerta, which led him to take sides. In retaliation for the seizure of an American by a body of Huerta's men he ordered the navy to seize the port of Vera Cruz which was duly done. This, of course, weakened Huerta owing to his difficulty in obtaining supplies from overseas. His power began to ebb, and such was the Mexican situation, with the Americans well and truly involved, when the First World War broke out.

7 The Last Years of Peace

IT WOULD BE UNREALISTIC to suggest that the death of King Edward VII on 6 May 1910 represented a turning-point in the national life of his country. It neither opened the way to fresh currents nor diverted the course of those that were already in motion. A new world, which both socially and politically would have been unrecognisable by the great Victorians, had been coming into existence before his accession, and had shown its characteristics strongly enough while he was still on the throne. Moreover, in the last four years of his life domestic politics, culminating in the struggle over the powers of the House of Lords, and foreign affairs, growing ever more restless and uneasy, had already disturbed some men's minds with the sense that the foundations, as well as the surface, of a long-familiar world were crumbling.

Yet in retrospect it is impossible to resist the conclusion that even if it be admitted that the year 1910 was no turning-point it does seem to associate itself with an unwelcome change in the country's state of mind. From such beginnings as serious strikes unauthorised by the Trade Union leaders, the early demonstrations of the new movement for women's suffrage, and the platform extravagances of the 1909 Budget campaign, it grew until a temper of sheer fighting seemed to invade every aspect of affairs, working up to the verge of civil war in 1914. The traditional Englishman, with his love of compromise, appeared to have become a relic of the past. It would not be fanciful to detect a similar development in other spheres than political. In art (though in this field the attack upon old conventions has always been marked by a considerable amount of intolerance), the new methods of painting, the new conceptions of the stage were all more or less lurid – certainly violence of expression was an essential component. In social life the old steady penetration of the world of fashion by the world of wealth, only too pleased to maintain the old barriers once it was safely inside them, was giving place to a feverish, contemptuous construction of a new world of fashionable idleness, well attuned to a world of lurid art. Industry more and more took on the aspect of two massed opposed forces, and between them compromise became even more precarious. The result was that the period between King Edward's death and the outbreak of the First World War consisted of very militant years.

Not understanding the world situation, either political or economic, the mass of the British people thought that they could afford the luxury of quarrelling among themselves, and this they proceeded to do with a bitterness unknown since the late twenties and early thirties of the previous century: the bitterness, it may be added, increased as the Liberal government after 1906 took the first tentative steps towards the Welfare State. In consequence politics at King Edward's death were ceasing to be what they had been at his accession, namely a conflict of genuine principles dividing society vertically, with all classes represented on both sides, and were becoming a conflict between classes, whose divisions were determined by self-interest rather than by their estimate of the common good. The immediate consequence was to make some strange bed-fellows, for the merchant-bankers and the shipping interests, anxious about Free Trade, found themselves allied with the popular party in support of a government which kept its majority in the House of Commons together by fighting the battle of

66 London 1911. During the coronation festivities King George V and Queen Mary drove in procession down Fleet Street on their way to the Guildhall.

Welsh Nonconformity and Irish Home Rule, and which was making some very attractive promises to the proletariat.

On the other side were mainly the squirearchy, then a very important factor in the national life, the county towns, and the professional classes, as well as the large section of the population which was opposed to Home Rule, and those whom Joseph Chamberlain had fired with his Imperialist theories.

It has been shown on an earlier page that the first General Election of 1910 raised more problems than it solved. The difficulty of the position was realised by some members of the government, and the Prime Minister informed the King, still Edward VII, that a section of the Cabinet was of the opinion that 'in view of the exorbitant demands of John Redmond [the Irish leader] and his followers, and the impossibility under existing Parliamentary conditions of counting upon a stable Government majority, the wisest and most dignified course for Ministers was at once to tender their resignation to Your Majesty'. The Irish, in effect, were prepared to vote for the Budget, but they demanded a Parliamentary assurance that once it was passed legislation would immediately be introduced to remove the veto of the House of Lords so that a measure of Home Rule could be carried, if necessary, over the head of that body. Redmond was told he could turn the government out if he dared, which he could not afford to do, as Asquith knew very well, and with the Opening of Parliament in February 1910 the conflict entered upon a new phase.

Once Asquith had made up his mind not to resign he lost no time in rallying a majority. On 21 March he tabled three resolutions: the first declared it expedient that the House of Lords should be prevented from rejecting or amending money Bills; the second stipulated that if a Bill passed the Commons in three successive Sessions, and was thrice rejected by the Lords, it should 'become law without the consent of the House of Lords on the Royal assent being declared'; and the third limited the duration

99

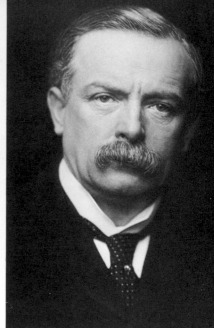

67 H. H. Asquith (1852–1928), the British Prime Minister, pays off his taxi-driver during the railway strike of 1911. He was noted for his dignity and indifference to personal attack, but was manœuvred out of office in 1916.

68 David Lloyd George (1863–1945) in 1912 – a brilliant, controversial statesman and radical reformer, noted for his powers of oratory, destined to succeed Asquith in 1916.

of any one Parliament to five years, thus modifying the Septennial Act of 1716, and the Prime Minister then introduced a Bill founded on them. Meanwhile, negotiations had been taking place with Redmond, as a result of which a few changes were made in the Finance Bill to render it more palatable to Ireland, and as the House of Lords made no further resistance this became law at the end of April. The stage was now set for the second round in which the Liberal government, supported by the Irish and Labour Parties, was ranged against the House of Lords, backed by the Conservative Opposition.

The ranging shots were fired in the last days of King Edward's life, for Asquith was clearly toying with the idea of asking the Sovereign to create enough peers to force the Parliament Bill through the Upper House. A week before his death, however, the King had received a notification to the effect that Balfour would be prepared to form a government in order to prevent him 'being put in the position contemplated by the demand for the creation of peers'. Unfortunately, not realising that death was so near, King Edward did not pass this information on to the Prince of Wales.

To King Edward VII there succeeded King George V, and few men could have been more dissimilar than this father and son. The new monarch lacked any sort of charm, while he knew little, and appeared to care less, about those international problems which so fascinated his two immediate predecessors on the throne. A professional sailor, he knew next to nothing of the world outside the Royal Navy, save perhaps where shooting and philately were concerned. He was to turn out a good, if not remarkable, and patriotic King, with a number of qualities which were very useful in the difficult circumstances of his reign, though it was some time before this fact became known to his subjects, and one of the leading journalists of the day, Kennedy Jones, undoubtedly expressed the view of a good many people when he wrote to Garvin, for so long Editor of *The Observer*, on the morrow of the old King's death, 'I have no great faith in George. Those who know him tell me he lacks charm of manner and broad human sympathies.'

The accession of King George V diverted public attention from political controversy, and when the ceremonies connected with it and the funeral of his predecessor were over there was a general feeling that it would be most unfair to confront the new monarch with a constitutional crisis. If the politicians could arrive at a compromise between themselves, so argued the ordinary citizen, who took any interest in the matter at all, it would be better for everybody. Accordingly, the Prime Minister proposed to Balfour that four of the leading men on either side should meet in conference with a view to finding a solution acceptable to both parties. The Opposition leader agreed to the proposal, and Asquith nominated to represent the government, in addition to himself, Crewe, Lloyd George, and Birrell, while Balfour chose Lansdowne, Cawdor and Austen Chamberlain. To this day it is not easy to decide whether the Prime Minister really wanted a compromise or whether he was merely playing for time, though there would appear to be little doubt that Lloyd George was sincerely desirous of an agreement.

The conference met for the first time on 17 June 1910 and it continued to sit with interruptions until 10 November, holding twenty-two meetings in all. On 11 November it was announced that the conference had broken up without reaching an agreement, though nothing was said as to the cause of its failure. Asquith now decided to force the pace, so he told the King that he wanted an immediate dissolution of Parliament; when asked his reasons, in view of the fact that the existing Parliament was still very young and that he had a good majority, Asquith, who was in a 'very bullying mood', to quote the King's own words, said that it was to pass the Veto Bill as the Liberals were ready for an election while the Conservatives were unprepared for one. After some further discussion, not of the most amicable nature it would appear, a compromise was reached by which the Sovereign promised the dissolution, but only after the Veto Bill had been submitted to the Lords, while he flatly refused at this stage to give any pledge as to the creation of peers.

On 15 November Parliament met, and the Veto Bill was introduced in the House of Lords. Its terms were that, pending a reform of the composition of the Upper Chamber, any measure which passed the Commons in three successive sessions unchanged might be presented for the Royal Assent without the consent of the Lords; and that any financial measures might be put before the King in the same way if, at the end of a month, the Lords' consent was withheld. The government did not wait for the Bill to be defeated, for a week after the failure of the conference the announcement of the coming dissolution of Parliament was made. In making it Asquith declared that the Ministers would not have advised it except on such conditions that if successful at the polls they would be able to place the Bill upon the Statute Book despite the resistance of the House of Lords. This could only mean that in the event of victory, and if the House of Lords still refused to give way, Ministers had received from the Sovereign an assurance that sufficient peers would be created to ensure the passage of the Bill into law.

There was another course which might, with perfect constitutional propriety, have been taken, and which it would appear that King Edward had envisaged, and that was to entrust Balfour with the formation of an administration: that this was not done was almost wholly due to Knollys, the King's Private Secretary, who was a strong Liberal, and who seems to have placed his sympathy with the government before his loyalty to his master. He knew perfectly well that the Leader of the Opposition would, however unwillingly, be prepared to take office, but he deliberately allowed the Sovereign to conclude that this was not the case. Three years were to elapse before the King realised that he had been duped, and he then dictated and initialled a note to the effect that had he known the truth it would have had an important bearing and influence with regard to Asquith's request for guarantees to create peers. Balfour always considered that Knollys had behaved extremely badly, not only to the King but also to himself. He was, as he had shown when Prime Minister, an easy-going man, but when he was asked by the late Lady Desborough whom he would like to meet or not to meet on a proposed week-end visit to her house at Taplow, he replied, 'My dear Ettie, I should enjoy meeting any man in England except Lord Knollys: him I will not meet.'

Had the King appealed to the Opposition a General Election would, in view of the state of parties in the House of Commons, have been necessary, but the result might have been very different: the party in power has always a great advantage in such circumstances in that it can decide the issue upon which the election is fought: Balfour would have placed the stress upon Home Rule, which the electorate had twice rejected, rather than upon the iniquities of the House of Lords, and in that case the verdict of the polls might have been very different. Had he been defeated the House of Lords must have accepted the verdict, and the threat to swamp that body by the creation of new peers would not have been necessary. In effect, whichever way the nation voted, the crisis of the following year would have been avoided.

In the event the General Election of December 1910 decided nothing. No less than 87 per cent of those who were in a position to vote did so, as compared with 92 per cent in the previous January, and there were returned 240 Conservatives, 34 Liberal Unionists, 270 Liberals, 42 Labour, and 84 Irish Nationalists. The deadlock was complete, and it was clear that no useful purpose would be served by any fresh appeal to the electorate. In another way, too, the verdict was extremely unsatisfactory, for the fact that the Conservatives and Unionists were slightly superior in numbers to the Liberals encouraged their Right Wing, under the name of Die-Hards, to oppose the Veto Bill to the uttermost, and for several months it looked as if the King might be called upon to fulfil his promise to create enough peers to ensure the passage of the measure through the Upper House.

The new Parliament met on 6 February 1911, and on the 21st the Prime Minister introduced the Veto Bill. For the next six months tempers at Westminster became steadily more inflamed, but in spite of this it is necessary to remember that the constitutional crisis of 1911 was in no sense a national crisis, for the nation as a whole took little interest in it.

Also there were many things to distract public attention from politics, for this was Coronation year, and, incidentally, one of the warmest of the century. As a preliminary spectacle the German Emperor made what was to be his last appearance in London in May at the formal opening of the Queen Victoria Memorial with the New Mall and the Admiralty Arch. The actual Coronation took place on 22 June, in perfect weather, and on the following day the King and Queen drove through miles of London streets.

69   The procession of an Indian dignitary at the Great
Delhi Durbar. On this occasion George V announced that
the capital of India was to be transferred from Calcutta to Delhi.

In July the Prince of Wales was officially invested at Caernarvon, and later in the year his father and mother took their departure for India for the Delhi Durbar. Pageantry broke out in the theatre too, for a taste for barbaric Orientalism brought Reinhardt's Arabian Night *Sumurum* to London, and Oscar Asche followed it with the spectacular display of *Kismet*. The potentialities of flying were beginning to be discussed; it was two years since Blériot had flown the Channel, but in 1911 there took place the first non-stop flight from London to Paris.

Unhappily there was another side to the picture, and that was the growing industrial unrest, frequently marked by violence. At Hull, Cardiff, and Manchester there was fighting in the streets, while in the last-named city the forces of law and order had to be augmented by a strong body of London police and by a detachment of the Scots Greys from the garrison at York. These particular strikes were, indeed, settled, but hardly had this taken place before there were the most violent scenes in Liverpool, where two men were shot and two hundred people injured, and at Llanelly, where again two were shot and four were killed by the explosion of a petrol tank. Lastly, in August there took place the first national railway strike, but this was a good deal less of a fiasco for motor transport was beginning to make its influence felt.

Abroad it was the year of the Agadir crisis and of the declaration of war by Italy upon Turkey as described on an earlier page.

While these events were taking place the Veto Bill, having been forced through the Commons, reached the Upper House in May. Earlier that month Lansdowne, on behalf of the Opposition, had produced yet another scheme for the reform of the House of Lords, and for this prospectively reformed chamber he proceeded to attempt to retain power by amendments to the Veto Bill: the most important of these provided for a Joint

70   London, 1911. Strikers march over the Willesden
railway bridge during the first great railway strike in
Britain.

Committee of both Houses in cases of disagreement, and reserved for a Referendum
such Bills as those establishing national Parliaments, by which Home Rule for Ireland
was implied, or raising issues of great gravity which clearly meant the Disestablishment
of the Welsh Church. Asquith would naturally have none of these amendments, and
such being the case the question at once arose whether the Opposition majority in the
House of Lords would insist on them, and thus force the creation of peers upon the
unhappy King. The issue was not at once joined, for there was a political truce over
the Coronation, but on 21 July a letter from the Prime Minister to Balfour was published
stating that the Commons would be asked to disagree with the Lords' amendments; it
proceeded: 'In the circumstances, should the necessity arise, the Government will advise
the King to exercise his Prerogative to secure the passing into law of the Bill in substantially the same form in which it left the House of Commons, and His Majesty has been
pleased to signify that he will consider it his duty to accept and act on that advice.'

This letter was the occasion of one of the stormiest scenes in British Parliamentary
history, for when, on 24 July, Asquith rose to move the rejection of the Lords' amendments, and to make his statement, the Opposition refused him a hearing. He was
howled down, and the Speaker adjourned the House without the question put. 'The
ugliest feature', Winston Churchill, then a Liberal, wrote to the King, 'was the absence
of any real passion or spontaneous feeling. It was a squalid, organised attempt to insult
the Prime Minister.' All the same a solution was very near, for on the following day
another letter was published, this time from Balfour to Lord Newton, advising the
House of Lords to accept the original Bill and to abandon their amendments. The
advice was taken on 10 August, at the close of one of the hottest days of that very hot
summer, for during the day the thermometer had registered 100, and the Bill was
passed by 131 votes to 114. Lansdowne and his followers abstained, but the government,
in addition to its own eighty supporters, received the votes of thirteen prelates and
thirty-seven Conservative peers. 'We were beaten', declared George Wyndham, 'by the
Bishops and the Rats', while *The Observer* denounced, 'The ignoble band, clerical and
lay, of Unionist traitors, who had made themselves Redmond's helots.' The first great

crisis of the reign was over, and the Throne had been treated by both parties as if it were a mere pawn in the political game.

The year 1911 may also be said to have witnessed the commencement of the militant suffragette activities. At the decennial census some of the more determined ladies had given expression to their opinions by sleeping out on commons in order not to be included in the returns, and in November a number of them burst upon the West End streets, smashing club and shop windows indiscriminately. They got no sympathy from the government, for when a deputation of them was received by Asquith he told them bluntly, 'Get rid of me if you can, but I am head of the Government, and I am not convinced.' The next two years witnessed an intensification of the violence, for another outburst of window-breaking was rapidly followed by serious pillar-box outrages, the partial destruction by a bomb of a house in building for Lloyd George at Walton Heath, the burning of two or three railway-stations near London, the systematic mutilation of golf greens, and the cutting of telegraph and telephone wires. In the Derby of 1913 a suffragette threw herself under a horse, and was so crushed that she died within a few hours. Whether these tactics advanced or retarded the cause of women's suffrage with the general public is a moot point.

On 15 April 1912 came the appalling news that the White Star liner *Titanic* had been sunk in mid-Atlantic on her maiden voyage, with the loss of 1,635 lives. What made the disaster more terrible was the advance publicity to the effect that such a thing could not happen. She was a ship of 46,000 tons, and she had been described as so huge that the sea, so far from endangering her, could scarcely even disturb the comfort of life aboard: passengers need not know, if they did not wish, that they were at sea at all; now one single iceberg across her track in the night had dispelled all these illusions. There was more in the shock, too, than the heavy loss of life; such a disaster was a terrible reminder to a generation growing ever more confident of its command over nature and the material world.

71   A suffragette is arrested after chaining herself to the railings of Buckingham Palace. The suffrage campaign was to achieve partial success in 1918, but it was not until 1928 that all women over twenty-one received the vote.

Another sensation which occurred at this time was of a very different nature, namely the so-called 'Marconi Scandal'. The Imperial Conference which met in 1911 had recommended the construction of a chain of wireless stations within the Empire, and in the following year Herbert Samuel, then Postmaster-General, accepted the tender put forward by the Marconi Company subject to ratification by Parliament. The shares of the Marconi Company, which in July 1911 were at forty shillings, had risen by April 1912 to eight pounds, and the Managing Director was Godfrey Isaacs, brother of the Attorney-General, Rufus Isaacs. During the summer recess rumours began to circulate that certain members of the government had speculated in Marconi shares, and in October in the House of Commons George Lansbury hinted that certain Ministers had used their previous knowledge of the government's intentions to indulge in 'disgraceful, scandalous, gambling in these shares'. Rufus Isaacs, speaking from the front bench, denied having had 'one single transaction with the shares of that company'. All the same, the government then appointed a Select Committee to inquire into the tender in its technical aspects, and at the same time to investigate the allegations that had been made.

At the beginning of April 1913 the matter was carried a little further when Asquith had an audience of the King, and told him – somewhat belatedly, one would have thought – that at the beginning of the year the Master of Elibank (the Chief Liberal Whip), Rufus Isaacs, and Lloyd George had admitted to him that, although they had had no dealings in the shares of the British Marconi Company, they had in fact bought some in its American counterpart. Realising that these facts would now be disclosed, they feared that they might be placed in a terribly awkward position, and offered their resignations: Asquith, possibly unduly magnanimously, refused to accept them; but he considered their conduct 'lamentable in itself, and so difficult to defend'.

The truth came out when Rufus Isaacs, together with Herbert Samuel (who was totally ignorant of the transactions of his colleagues), brought a libel action against the *Matin* newspaper, for on that occasion Isaacs admitted that he and two of his friends had dealt in the shares of the American Marconi Company. The Select Committee reported in June, and exonerated the Ministers from all charges of corruption; but in a minority report Lord Robert Cecil accused them of having committed a 'grave impropriety' and of having been 'wanting in frankness and respect for the House of Commons'. In the debate that followed, Asquith contended that his colleagues had not departed from 'rules of obligation', although they had certainly deviated from 'those of prudence'. The House then passed a resolution clearing the Ministers on the charge of corruption, and accepting their expressions of regret.

One of the centres of unrest was Westminster. The Opposition considered that the methods employed to put the Veto Bill upon the Statute Book, as well as the Bill itself, had strained the Constitution almost to breaking-point, and that in consequence they were justified in adopting tactics which might otherwise not have been admissible. Smarting under the loss of three General Elections the Conservatives felt that Tierney's famous definition of the duty of an Opposition admirably fitted their own case, namely to propose nothing, to oppose everything, and to turn out the government. No handle against the administration was to be neglected, and this explains why such measures as the Insurance Bill, which in retrospect appears almost non-contentious, were so fiercely attacked. The man-in-the-street did not take all this very seriously, though he was

72   John Redmond (1856–1918) at the House of Commons.
After January 1910 his Irish party held the balance of power
in the Chamber.

certainly more interested in politics at that time than he was later to become, and it
must be confessed that from the spectacular point of view politics had much to recommend them. On the government's side a speech by Lloyd George or Winston Churchill
was always good value in vituperation and personalities, while it could be relied upon
within a few days to produce, on the part of the Opposition, a retort by Carson or
F. E. Smith couched in similar language: those who preferred to see controversy carried
on at a higher level had their choice of Asquith or Balfour. Indeed, political warfare was
almost gladiatorial, and the mass of the electorate liked it that way.

    With the coming of the year 1912 the shadow of Ireland began to lengthen over
British politics, and the United States' Ambassador, Walter H. Page, was remarking
'Somehow it reminds me of the tense days of the slavery controversy, just before the
Civil War.' To understand why this should have been the case it is necessary to go back
to the beginning of the century.

    When Queen Victoria died it seemed as if the old bitterness was disappearing from
Irish politics: gone were the days of 'buckshot' Forster and 'bloody' Balfour, and in their
place was a sweet reasonableness on the part of the British which seemed to have
become wedded to a policy of killing Home Rule by kindness, forgetful of the fact that
down the ages the desire for autonomy has rarely been exorcised by material prosperity.
Nearer home Arthur Griffith had begun to publish *The United Irishman*: the Irish
Dramatic Movement had been launched; John Redmond had been elected Chairman
of the reunited Irish Parliamentary Party; and the census of 1901 gave the figure of
4,447,085 as the population.

    The man who was apparently indicated as the harbinger of the new dawn was no
less a person than the new Chief Secretary, George Wyndham, and at first he possessed
every qualification for the post. He was on the right side of forty; he was a scholar and
a gentleman; and he was an enthusiast for Ireland and all things Irish. He was un-

undoubtedly one of the most brilliant men who have ever appeared on the British political stage, but his very brilliance kept him apart from the mass of his colleagues in the House of Commons. In private he was the best of company, but few knew him in such intimate surroundings, and it cannot be denied that he suffered for his genius in that it cut him off from the rank-and-file of his own party. He thus by nature and circumstances tended to be out of touch with current opinion, and he was inclined to take it for granted that the mental processes of others were rapid as his own. Balfour complained that Wyndham was obscure. 'I wonder why', he once remarked to Austen Chamberlain. 'For one thing he talks in metaphors. I believe it's his natural way of talking, but it's a great bore for a person with a non-literary mind like mine.'

As ever, the outstanding Irish problem was the land, and to this Wyndham at once addressed himself: after one fatal start he achieved success, with a Land Act which Redmond rightly hailed as 'the most substantial victory gained for centuries by the Irish race for the reconquest of the soil of Ireland by the people'. Unhappily in this clear sky there was a small cloud which was to grow until it covered the whole horizon.

In the autumn of 1902 Sir Antony MacDonnell was appointed Under-Secretary for Ireland with special powers. Nothing could be argued against him on the score of competence or of his record as Governor of Bengal, but he was a Liberal in politics and a Roman Catholic by religion, and his brother was Nationalist M.P. for Queen's County. Unionist suspicions of Wyndham's intentions, never far beneath the surface, increased, and they were certainly not diminished by the widespread rumours that the Chief Secretary was much under the influence of the new Under-Secretary. The Land Act had been intended by Wyndham, MacDonnell, and those who thought with them as the beginning, but the more extreme Unionists, particularly in the North, intended that it should be an end, and when the Chief Secretary showed a disposition to deal in the same spirit with the demand for a Catholic university he was soon made to realise

73   July 1914. Irish Nationalist gun-runners at Howth, near Dublin. This month a consignment of 2,500 rifles was landed from Germany.

that he had gone too far. The Marquess of Londonderry, the President of the Board of Education, announced at the beginning of 1904 that the government had no intention of introducing any such measure, and soon afterwards Wyndham had to state openly that he had not been able to commit the Cabinet to his own views on the subject.

Meanwhile a number of the more progressive landlords, under the inspiration of Lord Dunraven, had been endeavouring to find a way round the Home Rule impasse, and had formed for this purpose an organisation called the Irish Reform Association. Dunraven, it may be added, worked closely with MacDonnell and both men firmly believed that Wyndham shared their views. In September 1904 the Reform Association produced a long manifesto proposing the creation of an Irish Financial Council, partly nominated and partly elective, and the establishment by Parliament of a statutory body to deal with such Irish affairs as were considered unsuitable for the attention of the Imperial Parliament. From the beginning it was clear that the Association's proposals did not go far enough to please one section of Irish opinion, while they went far too far for the other; Redmond himself was not unsympathetic, but Dillon saw in it the discreditable climax of a long campaign to kill Home Rule with kindness, and Davitt denounced it at once as a 'wooden horse stratagem'. On the other side Sir Edward Carson, Attorney-General for Ireland, publicly referred to the scheme as 'a gross betrayal', and declared that 'he preferred the repeal of the Union to any such tampering'.

Wyndham was in London when the storm broke, and as Parliament was in recess he took the somewhat unusual course for a Minister of writing a letter to *The Times* in which he repudiated all knowledge of the Irish Reform Association. If he hoped that this would ease his difficulties he was soon mistaken, for he was now further accused of having made a scapegoat of his Under-Secretary. His position had clearly become impossible, and at the beginning of March 1905 he resigned. By this time the Conservatives were tottering to a fall, and little of interest occurred where Ireland was concerned during the next few months, and in December there came a change of government.

This, however, soon proved to have made little difference to Ireland. Long experience had shown to the Irish that there was nothing to choose between the two English parties, and Redmond well put their point of view when he said, 'The sooner that the government understands that to us Whig, Tory, Liberal, Conservative, are but as names, and that British governments are judged by us by what they do and not by their professions of sympathy, the better it will be for them and for every one concerned.' Mindful of their defeats in 1886 and 1895 on the subject of Home Rule the Liberal leaders were fearful of introducing any measure with that end in view, and as they possessed an independent majority in the House of Commons they were under no necessity of placating Redmond and his followers: they went, however, so far as to introduce a Bill to establish an Irish Council having wide administrative powers but with no power to make laws or to control finance. This emasculated form of Home Rule was referred by the Irish Party to a Convention in Dublin, which contemptuously flung it back in the Liberal government's face.

There was, however, another Ireland – the Ireland of the future – coming into existence, and in more ways than one it was a reaction against Lords-Lieutenant, Chief Secretaries, political action at Westminster, and all that these things implied. While the old Queen was still on the throne Arthur Griffith had started Sinn Fein and Douglas Hyde had founded the Gaelic League, and to them turned the young people who felt themselves frustrated by the fact that Irish ambitions had so obviously become the plaything of English politicians. The more far-seeing members of the Irish Parliamentary Party realised that there was no time to lose, and the two General Elections of 1910 having placed Asquith's government at their mercy they remorselessly applied the pressure. Accordingly a Home Rule Bill was introduced in the House of Commons in April 1912.

At once the question of the exclusion of the northern counties arose, and Carson, who was not an Ulsterman at all but a Dublin barrister, proposed an amendment to exclude the province of Ulster from the operation of the Home Rule Bill, and Redmond replied with the phrase, 'Ireland is for us one entity. It is one land.' Carson's amendment was defeated in the House of Commons, and the Third Reading of the Bill was duly carried, only, however, as had been foreseen, to be rejected by the House of Lords. This meant that the Bill would return to the Lower House, pass through all its stages again, and eventually be forced through both Houses by the operation of the Parliament Act: it was thus bound to become law by the summer of 1914. On 12 March 1913, in the debate on the Address, the Opposition moved an amendment to the effect that it would be improper to proceed with the Home Rule Bill 'while the constitution of Parliament is still incomplete and without reference to the electors'. In supporting this motion Bonar Law, Balfour's successor as Leader of the Opposition, contended that a law passed under such conditions 'could not, and ought not to, command respect and obedience'. The ranging shots had been fired.

Few people who were not alive at the time can have any idea of the extent to which the issue of Home Rule split the United Kingdom in the years 1913–14. The two islands were much more closely connected socially in those days than is now the case, and that at all levels. All over Ireland 'the big house' still stood, and English visitors who partook of its hospitality for hunting, shooting, and fishing were very numerous, while at the other end of the scale the Irish working class in such cities as Liverpool, Manchester, and Glasgow were an important political factor. Members of the opposing parties began to refuse to meet each other socially.

It soon became clear that the contest could not be confined to words alone, for the Ulster Protestants began to arm. By September 1913 the strength of the Ulster Volunteers was 56,000, and by March of the following year the figure had risen to 84,000. Arrangements were made for the accommodation in English country-houses of refugees from Ireland, and for the evacuation to England of the wounded in the civil war which loomed so ominously ahead. Not unnaturally the Irish Catholics also began to take action of a similar nature, and at a meeting held at the Rotunda in Dublin in November 1913 the National Volunteers were duly inaugurated. To complicate matters still further James Larkin, the Labour leader, started to enrol a force called the Irish Citizen Army, and for the purpose of training it he secured the assistance of an Ulster Protestant in the person of J. R. White, the son of the defender of Ladysmith.

Meanwhile, the King, undeterred by the rebuffs which he had met during the crisis over the Parliament Act, was endeavouring behind the scenes during the summer and autumn of 1913 to effect a compromise, and he had conversations with a number of prominent statesmen, but no real headway was made. He also persuaded Asquith to have some private discussions with Bonar Law, but they led to nothing.

The beginning of 1914 thus witnessed a deadlock, but in actual fact the situation was even worse than appeared on the surface, for the Opposition was encouraging the army to refuse to obey orders if it were directed to march against Ulster. At the beginning of February the King warned the Prime Minister that if civil war broke out many officers would resign their commissions rather than fight. 'But whom,' Asquith asked airily, 'are they going to fight?' In the latter part of March there occurred the 'Curragh incident', when a number of cavalry officers took exactly the line that the Sovereign had forecast, and which confirmed the worst of his apprehensions, with the result that for a brief space the country was brought to a realisation of the fact that it was on the edge of a catastrophe. The government speedily announced that it had never intended to coerce Ulster by force, and as a further measure of assurance Asquith took over the War Office in addition to the Premiership. 'All is the same as before', the King wrote in his diary, 'so the danger for the moment is over.'

Never was optimism more misplaced. On the night of 24–25 April the Ulster Volunteers were mobilised, and succeeded without interference in landing at Larne a consignment of twenty-five thousand rifles and three million rounds of ammunition. The fat was once more in the fire, and the King, having secured the promise of the Speaker to take the chair, urged the Prime Minister to consent to an all-party conference; twice he refused, but in the middle of July he changed his opinion, and said that after consultation with his colleagues he had come to the conclusion that it was his duty to advise the Sovereign, 'before the crisis became acute, to intervene with the object of securing a pacific accommodation'.

On the morning of 21 July a conference duly met at Buckingham Palace, and it was composed of Asquith and Lloyd George; Lansdowne and Bonar Law; Redmond and Dillon; Carson and Craig. They were received by the King, who welcomed each of them separately; after this the members of the conference took their seats round the Council Room table. The Sovereign was in the chair, but after a brief preliminary address he vacated it for the Speaker; and left the room.

The intervention of the Crown was not destined to be successful. On 24 July the

74   A hunt starting off in the Mall, Waterford, in Ireland.

Prime Minister announced in the House of Commons that the conference had been unable to come to any agreement 'either in principle or in detail'. It seemed impossible to avoid catastrophe, for in a few weeks the Home Rule Bill would become law. Two days after Asquith had spoken the Nationalists landed a big consignment of arms near Howth. Such was the state of British politics when, on 28 July, the Foreign Secretary rose in the House of Commons to make a statement concerning the Austrian rejection of Serbia's reply to an ultimatum demanding satisfaction for the murder of the Archduke Franz Ferdinand.

The King's intervention had thus, through no fault of his own, been as great a failure in 1914 in the case of Ireland as in 1910–11 in respect of the Constitution. On both occasions one of the principal causes had been his inexperience and the lack of weight which he carried. The power and prestige of a British monarch grows the longer he or she is on the throne, and King George V had only recently succeeded his father, while for a variety of reasons he was none too popular. Where Ireland was concerned he suffered, like so many Englishmen, from the delusion that he understood the country, and he interpreted the warmth of his reception in Dublin after the Coronation to mean that the Royal Family was popular as such. That Ireland is fundamentally a conservative country is true, and there was much to be said for Arthur Griffith's solution of the problem of her relations with Great Britain, namely a Dual Monarchy on the Austro-Hungarian pattern, but King George was not the man to play that hand as it would have had to be played. His heart was unquestionably in the right place, but he was fundamentally rather a stupid man, and in the years immediately preceding the First World War he had not acquired the experience of affairs which was later to compensate for his slowness in the uptake. His intentions were excellent, but excellent intentions were not enough by themselves to solve the Irish Question. What course British history would have taken had war not broken out, and what part the monarchy would have played, it is quite impossible to conjecture.

With the outbreak of war Home Rule went into cold storage. The Bill itself was put on the Statute Book, but attached to it was a suspensory measure preventing its operation until peace came. Long before then the future of Ireland was being settled by the bullet rather than the ballot-box.

The history of Scotland, on the contrary, during the first fourteen years of the twentieth century was much more peaceful, and public opinion was more concerned with religious than with political or social problems with the centripetal forces gaining ground, especially where the non-Established Presbyterian Churches were concerned. The Free Church had been joined as far back as 1876 by the bulk of the Reformed Presbyterians or Cameronians, and now, after a quarter of a century, negotiations with the United Presbyterian Church were resumed, with the result that in 1900 the Free Church and the United Presbyterian Church became one under the name of the United Free Church. The Free Church, it is to be noted, had had experience that, since it broke away from the Established Church of Scotland at the Disruption in 1843, though it 'went out' to secure its spiritual independence from the interference of the civil courts, these courts never hesitated to adjudicate upon any case brought by a minister or member alleging breach of contract against the Church; it therefore took a great risk as a Church which had hitherto maintained the 'establishment principle' when it united with a confessedly voluntary body.

75　Glasgow Bridge, looking south from Jamaica Street,
April 1914.

In these circumstances it is not surprising that some thirty of its ministers and a certain proportion of its members refused to enter the Union, and became colloquially known as 'Wee Frees'. Cross-actions were brought between the uniting majority and the dissentient minority, and both parties asked to be declared the rightful holder in trust of the Free Church property. The Scottish courts decided in favour of the majority, but in 1904 the House of Lords reversed this decision. Their lordships held that by passing a certain Declaratory Act in which the doctrine of the Confession had been modified, and by ceasing to maintain the principle of an Established Church, the majority had ceased to represent the Free Church: in consequence the ministers and congregations who held to the ancient standards unmodified were declared to be the Free Church of Scotland, and thus entitled to hold its eleven hundred churches and other property both at home and abroad. In effect, the case had really turned on the point whether a Trust for a Church was a Trust to promulgate a rigid doctrine, or whether it might be a Trust for an organisation free to mould its own doctrine and its own constitution: the Law Lords had taken the former view.

This decision created an impossible situation, for the minority was manifestly unable to discharge its trust, so recourse was perforce had to Parliament. Accordingly the Scottish Churches Bill was introduced to give the Free Church the relief necessary to allow her to retain the bulk of her property, and there was no opposition to its provisions in principle. It was another thing, however, when to the same Bill a fifth clause was added, which dealt, not with the Free, but with the Established, Church of Scotland, empowering her without recourse to Parliament to alter the form of subscription to the Confession of Faith laid down in the Act of 1690. Campbell-Bannerman, then Leader of the Opposition, took strong exception to this; he described Clause V as an 'undesirable alien', a phrase which was highly topical at the moment owing to the

76 Fettes College, founded in 1870, one of the famous
Scottish schools.

controversy over the Aliens Act; and demanded that it should be introduced, if at all,
in a separate Bill.

This was just the sort of controversy in which Balfour, then Prime Minister,
delighted, and he took Clause V through Committee himself, declaring that it was 'no
intruder', but was relevant to the general interest of Presbyterianism in Scotland. The
Bill passed into law on 20 July 1903 and thus accorded a new-found liberty the General
Assembly of the Established Church in 1910 framed the formula, 'I hereby subscribe
the Confession of Faith, declaring that I accept it as the Confession of this Church,
and that I believe the fundamental doctrines of the Christian Faith contained therein.'

The essential justice of this action on the part of Parliament was generally admitted,
and by none more heartily than the members of the Church of Scotland. At the same
time, the case showed how futile it was to expect that a Church which holds property,
collects funds, and has a settled constitution can keep its affairs out of the civil courts,
if in any of its activities it may be held to infringe the rights of a minority or of an
individual.

However detrimental to the best religious interests of the country these dissensions
might be, there can be no doubt but that at the beginning of the twentieth century the
Churches still maintained their hold upon the people. In 1843, before the Disruption,
the communicants of the Church of Scotland did not number more than 14 per cent
of the population, but in 1908 they numbered nearly 15 per cent, while those of the
United Free Church were over 10 per cent: in other words, taken together they
amounted to 25 per cent, while their activities and their contributions were estimated
to have increased in a still greater proportion. To arrive at a figure for the practising

Christian inhabitants of the kingdom there must, of course, be added the communicating members of the Roman Catholic and Episcopalian Churches.

During the latter part of the nineteenth century there was an excessive amount of drunkenness in Scotland, and in the sixties it was estimated that in Edinburgh between 40 and 50 per cent of all those arrested by the police were drunk when they committed the crime for which they were taken into custody. The situation was, however, improving.

In 1907 a representative of the Board of Trade was sent to inquire into the prevalence of excessive drinking in the British Isles, and he found that drunkenness was definitely on the decrease in Scotland. 'Dundee', he wrote, 'was the worst place for drink; young women in the jute factories were wheeled home drunk in barrows on Saturday nights; and they were only paid 10s. a week. On the whole, however, it was clear that the abuse of alcohol and the money spent on it were rapidly decreasing all over the country, and that the population generally was much more sober than it had been ten years before.'

If there was much to criticise in the Scotland of those days, there was equally much to admire, and her system of education was still one of the wonders of the world; indeed it is no exaggeration to say that Scotland had a national system of education when England was merely groping in the dark. Some have held that as the twentieth century progressed Scotland tended to lag behind her southern neighbour, but this was certainly not the case in the years immediately preceding the First World War.

To pass from the particular to the general, that is to say from local affairs to national politics, one of the outstanding characteristics of Scottish life in the nineteenth century had been the popular devotion to the Liberal Party. At the General Election of 1880 of the sixty members returned by Scotland only seven were Conservatives: the position became modified when the split in the Liberal ranks over Home Rule took place, and when Salisbury appealed to the country in 1900 the proportion after the election of that year was thirty-eight Conservatives and Liberal Unionists to thirty-four Liberals: it was, however, a mere flash in the pan, for in 1906 there were returned a mere twelve Conservatives and Liberal Unionists to fifty-eight Liberals and two Labour. 'In Scotland', Austen Chamberlain wrote to Balfour, 'the class hatred was very bitter and the animosity against landlords extreme. Nothing else counted very much.' The two General Elections of 1910 made no material alteration in the political complexion of Scottish representation in the House of Commons.

Where Wales was concerned there was little unity in the earlier years of the present century, quite apart from the difference between the industrial South and the pastoral and agricultural North. The great division between Church and Chapel affected every social relationship, for to be a Nonconformist implied the profession of Liberalism and a belief in the infallibility of Lloyd George, while Churchmen were always Tories who considered him as an emanation of the infernal regions. The main bone of contention was the Church of Wales, and the Bill for its disestablishment was subject to much the same vicissitudes as that for Home Rule. It, also, was passed, but put into cold storage at the beginning of the First World War, though unlike the Irish measure it was put into operation when peace came.

8 The Coming of the First World War

THE RAPID DETERIORATION in the international situation has been described on an earlier page, and whatever hopes there may have been of the preservation of peace were destroyed by the murder on 28 June 1914 at Serajevo in Bosnia of the Archduke Franz Ferdinand, the heir to the Habsburg throne; this set in motion the events which culminated five weeks later in one of the greatest catastrophes civilisation has ever known. To what extent this crime was directly inspired by Belgrade is, perhaps, a moot point, but its immediate effect was to convince even the most moderate in Vienna that it was essential to administer a sharp lesson to Serbia. The attitude of Franz Josef, who had more than once in the past restrained his wild men, is well brought out in a letter which he sent to Kaiser Wilhelm a day or two after the murder:

> The crime against my nephew is the first consequence of the agitation carried on by Russian and Serbian Pan-Slavists, whose sole aim is to weaken the Triple Alliance and shatter my Empire. Though it may be impossible to prove the complicity of the Serbian government, there can be no doubt that its policy, intent on uniting all Jugoslavs under the Serbian flag, must encourage such crimes and endanger my house and countries if it is not stopped. My efforts must be directed to isolating Serbia, and reducing her size. After the recent terrible event I am certain that you also are convinced that agreement between Serbia and us is out of the question, and that the peace policy of all European monarchs is threatened so long as this centre of criminal agitation remains unpunished in Belgrade.

What had, in effect, happened was that the old strife between Teuton and Slav had broken out in a new form. If the Dual Monarchy became Triune, then in due course the Jugoslavs would look to Vienna rather than to Belgrade and St Petersburg; therefore Franz Ferdinand was murdered. On the other hand, as the German White Book put it, 'If the Serbs continued, with the aid of Russia and France, to menace the existence of Austria, her gradual collapse and the subjection of all the Slavs under the Russian sceptre would result, thus rendering untenable the position of the Teutonic race in Central Europe. A morally weakened Austria under the pressure of a Russian Pan-Slavism would be no longer an ally on whom we could count in view of the ever menacing attitude of our eastern and western neighbours.' Therefore Germany had to stand by her ally.

So far the situation was very much what it had been in 1908; Germany was ready to support Austria-Hungary, and Great Britain had certainly no intention of going to war for the sake of Serbia. On the other hand, the forces making for peace were everywhere weaker, especially in Vienna, than six years before, and Berchtold, who had succeeded Aehrenthal as Austro-Hungarian Foreign Minister in 1912, was far from possessing the diplomatic skill of his predecessor. Aehrenthal had refrained from putting any real pressure on Belgrade until he knew that Russia would not intervene, while Berchtold presented an ultimatum to Serbia in such circumstances that Russia was left with no alternative save to support her Serbian client. Instead, therefore, of following

77   The aged Emperor Franz Josef in 1914 at the age of
eighty-four. In old age he was a revered and tragic figure.
His wife and two heirs, son and nephew, had all died
violent deaths.

the precedent of 1908 Berchtold preferred that of 1859, when precipitate action was
taken with fatal consequences against Sardinia, and thus made his country appear in
the wrong, when, in fact, it had a very good case. In Berlin there were conflicting
counsels, so what Bismarck would never have allowed took place, the Austrian horse
bolted with the German waggon, and the Reich was forced into war with Russia.

It was also a tragedy that none of the Heads of State were, for one reason or
another, capable of riding the storm. King George V failed to take any personal
initiative, as his father would surely have done, but he can hardly be blamed since he
was still smarting under the rebuffs administered to him by the conferences on the
Veto Bill and the Irish Question, and he was determined to take care not to be
humiliated again. The French President, by this time Raymond Poincaré, was little
more than a bureaucrat. Had the Austrian Emperor been a younger man he would
have curbed the recklessness of his Foreign Office and his General Staff, and this in its
turn would have exercised a soothing influence upon Kaiser Wilhelm II, who, though
highly emotional, was pacific by nature. The most pathetic case of all was that of the
Tsar who was quite unable to exercise any control over his servants, for when he
ordered mobilisation against Austria-Hungary alone in the hope of thereby limiting the
scope of the conflict the War Minister continued with a general mobilisation, while
concealing the fact from his master, and denying it to the German military attaché.

On 23 July 1914 the Austrian ultimatum was presented at Belgrade with a time-
limit of forty-eight hours. The demands of Austria-Hungary, set out in ten articles,

117

included not only the suppression of Pan-Serbian societies and propaganda, but the co-operation of officials of the Dual Monarchy in the measures required for that purpose. From the beginning it was clear that everything turned on the attitude of Russia, and Grey told the Austro-Hungarian Ambassador that if the ultimatum did not lead to trouble with St Petersburg he had no concern with it, and he went so far as to urge Serbia to promise the fullest satisfaction if any of her officials should prove to have been accomplices in the Serajevo murder. The views of the Russian government were not long in doubt, and Sazonoff, the Foreign Minister, described the ultimatum as provocative and immoral, while the military party at St Petersburg was by no means averse from a conflict of which Constantinople might be the prize. With the clouds thus rapidly gathering, Grey suggested the cessation of all military operations pending a conference; and the Serbian acceptance of the ultimatum, save in the matter of the co-operation of foreign officials, afforded some slight hope that his efforts at mediation might be successful. Even at this late hour peace might have been preserved had Great Britain and Germany worked together as they had done during the recent Balkan crisis.

There was, however, no controlling hand in Berlin, as was shown at the Crown Council held on 29 July. The Chancellor, Bethmann-Hollweg, was himself strongly in favour of peace, but he had lost all control of the situation, and the Kaiser was vacillating; on the other side were those who said that a more favourable moment for war would never come, with Britain split from top to bottom on the Irish Question and the Russian army in the throes of reorganisation. Such being the case, it is not surprising that the worst was made of both worlds. There was an attempt to buy British neutrality on impossible terms, while Vienna was warned not to precipitate matters. Berchtold and his colleagues, with the full support of their fellow countrymen it may be added, however, took the line that operations against Serbia, which had already begun, must

78   Serajevo, 28 June 1914. The Archduke Franz Ferdinand and the Duchess Sophie about to board the car in which, one minute later, they were assassinated.

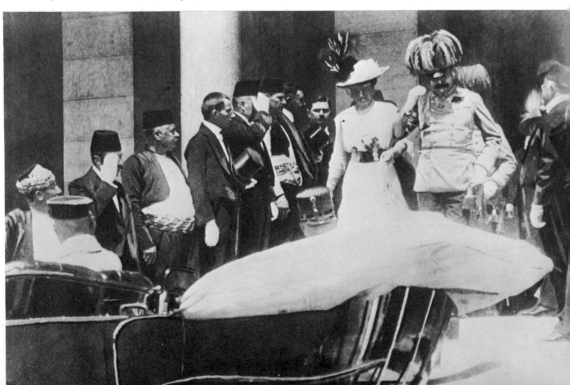

continue; that the British suggestion could not be adopted until the Russian mobilisation had ceased; and that the ultimatum must be accepted as a whole.

At first it was by no means certain where Great Britain herself would stand in the event of an outbreak of hostilities. The time had not yet come when, in moments of international crisis, Ministers took their opponents into their confidence, and the Opposition was largely dependent upon hearsay for information as to the progress of events. It was known that the Cabinet was overwhelmingly pacific, and in the event of intervention some seven or eight resignations were to be expected. Churchill communicated the feeling in inner Liberal circles to F. E. Smith, and asked for an assurance that if these resignations took place the vacancies would be filled by the Opposition leaders. Bonar Law, however, refused to entertain any advances that came from or through Churchill, whom he thoroughly mistrusted, and there the matter rested. So far as the Conservative Party was concerned the situation was further complicated by Balfour who, at dinner a few days earlier, had argued, not uncharacteristically, to Sir Arthur Nicolson, of the Foreign Office, against co-operation with France and Russia, the policy in which he really believed, for the sake of the dialectical exercise; Nicolson took him seriously, and reported what he thought were Balfour's views to Grey.

Asquith has left on record one last attempt that was made, on 1 August, to counteract the consequences of the behaviour of the Russian War Minister:

> When most of them [i.e. the Cabinet] had left, Sir W. Tyrrell arrived with a long message from Berlin to the effect that the German Ambassador's efforts for peace had been suddenly arrested and frustrated by the Tsar's decree for a complete Russian mobilisation. We all set to work, Tyrrell, Bongie [the late Sir Maurice Bonham-Carter], Drummond, and myself to draft a direct personal appeal from the King to the Tsar. When we had settled it I called a taxi, and in company with Tyrrell, drove to

79 Police seize one of the conspirators responsible for throwing the bomb. Princip and Čabrinović, the authors of the crime, belonged to a group of Bosnian Serb students who thought to solve by terrorism the problem of Austro-Hungarian repression in the Jugoslav provinces.

Buckingham Palace at about 1.30 a.m. The King was hauled out of bed, clad in a dressing-gown, while I read the message and the proposed answer.

Hostilities, however, were now inevitable, though, as Lloyd George was later to write, 'no one at the head of affairs quite meant war at that stage. It was something into which they glided, or rather staggered and stumbled, perhaps through folly.' On 31 July an ultimatum was sent from Berlin to St Petersburg demanding the cessation of mobilisation within twelve hours, and on the following day Germany and Russia were at war. On 3 August Germany declared war on France, and her troops crossed the Belgian frontier: this news put an end to the doubts and hesitations which had divided British opinion, and only two senior members of the government, Lord Morley and John Burns, resigned; an ultimatum was sent to Germany, demanding the withdrawal of her troops from Belgium, but no answer was returned, and midnight of 4–5 August marked the participation of Great Britain in the First World War.

The vicious circle was complete, and it is not the business of the historian to divide the belligerents into sheep and goats. From her own point of view Serbia was right in pursuing her national aims. Austria-Hungary was no less right in seeking to retain her possessions. It was the duty of Russia to fulfil her promises to Serbia. Germany was bound to try to prevent the forcible dissolution of her only trustworthy ally. France and Britain were compelled to honour their treaty obligations. Indeed, rightly to understand the causes of the First World War one has got to realise the truth of Hegel's profound aphorism, 'Tragedy is not the conflict of right and wrong, but of right with right.'

Though the conduct of each of the belligerents appeared to its enemies to indicate a double dose of original sin, it was nevertheless in every case what might have been expected. It was natural that Serbia should aspire to unite under her rule the discontented Jugoslav subjects of her neighbour, should use their undoubted grievances in Croatia to foster the Pan-Serb idea, and should look to Russia for assistance, as Cavour half a century earlier had looked to France in the creation of united Italy. It was equally natural that Austria-Hungary should be determined to defend herself against the openly proclaimed ambition to rob her of provinces which she had held for centuries. After the Bosnian crisis Serbia had promised to be a good neighbour, but she had not kept her word, and her intrigues with Russia were notorious. For the government in Vienna to sit with folded arms, and wait until its enemies felt strong enough to carry out their programme of dismemberment, was to proclaim impotence and invite disaster, while the murder of the Heir to the Throne appeared to be both a reason and an excuse to vindicate the authority of the Dual Monarchy. The ultimatum to Serbia appears in retrospect to have been a gambler's throw, but in Vienna and Budapest it was seen as a strictly defensive action which promised the best escape from a danger that was certain to increase until it threatened the very existence of Austria-Hungary.

The conduct of Germany was no less short-sighted, but no less intelligible. Austria had set her heart upon putting an end to the Serbian menace, and Austria was the only Power, large or small, on whom Germany could rely, for Italy and Romania were allies in nothing but name. If Austria ceased to be a Great Power through the loss of her southern provinces, Germany would stand alone in Europe, wedged in between a hostile Russia and a France bent on revenge for the loss of Alsace-Lorraine in the War of 1870. In the seventies Bismarck had bluntly told his Austrian ally that he would not fight for her Balkan ambitions; but in those far-off days Berlin had not lost touch with

80   Russian mobilisation. Cossacks on the march.

St Petersburg, and the Iron Chancellor also possessed the friendship of Britain which his successors had lost. At the same time Bismarck had repeatedly declared that the maintenance of Austria as a Great Power was a paramount interest for which Germans might fight with an easy conscience, and the policy of Berlin in 1908 had compelled Russia to keep the peace: such being the case, it was not unreasonable to suppose that a fresh demonstration of Austro-German solidarity might produce a similar result. If it did not the Central Powers felt themselves strong enough to defeat their enemies, for they knew that the Russian colossus had feet of clay, and France appeared quite unprepared for a struggle of life and death.

The German government was well aware of the risk of Great Britain taking the field by the side of France and Russia, which makes it all the more extraordinary that they should have rendered this inevitable by the invasion of Belgium. Above all, in Berlin a struggle between Teuton and Slav was considered to be almost inevitable sooner or later, and if it was to come the General Staff preferred 1914 to any subsequent date, when Russia's strategic railways on the Polish frontier would be complete and the Three Years' Service system in France would be in operation. It is true that the German navy had not yet reached its full stature, but the Kiel Canal had been deepened to take the largest battleships.

Basically, the main cause of the conflict lay in the Near East. 'I shall not see the world war', Bismarck observed to Ballin in 1891, 'but you will, and it will start in the East', and his prophecy came true. The situation in that part of the world meant little or nothing to France, but for a quarter of a century her destinies had been linked with those of Russia, and when the crisis came she took her place at the side of her partner. Her government had no desire for war, but equally no effort was made to restrain her ally. The fact was that France had never abandoned hope of recovering the Rhine provinces, and for that reason she was to be included among the 'restless Powers'. In the end she was dragged into war to sustain Russian prestige, and if she had declined the summons she would have found herself defenceless before Germany.

Italy stood aside, as everybody expected her to do, and for the greater part of a year *sacro egoismo* dictated her policy. Although she was nominally a member of the Triple Alliance her conduct had been extremely tortuous for a number of years. As far back as 1896 she had informed her allies that she could not fight on their side if Great Britain as well as France was among their enemies, and six years later she had pledged herself by treaty to take no part in an attack on France, while in 1909 she had promised her support for Russian ambitions in return for St Petersburg's support of her own: thus the summer of 1914 found her connected by treaties or understandings with every member of the Triple Entente. On the other hand, if Italy's relations with Germany were excellent the same could certainly not be said of those with Vienna, for it was only at the expense of Austria-Hungary that she could secure the Trentino, let alone Trieste and Fiume. In these circumstances no Italian statesman could have persuaded his countrymen to fight for the strengthening of Austria's position in the Balkans.

Finally, could any action on the part of Grey have averted war in 1914? Lloyd George in his later days asserted that had Germany been warned in time 'the issue would have been different'. Apart from the question to what extent Lloyd George was a reliable witness where Grey was concerned, the criticism can only mean that at some stage the Foreign Secretary could, by some action which he did not take, have averted the outbreak of hostilities. Looking back on the situation more than fifty years later it is clear that there was only one way in which war might have been prevented, and that was by giving firm notice to Germany that if she attacked France then she would find Britain in the field against her. This is possibly true, but it ignores the fact that there would not have been the necessary support either in the Cabinet or the House of Commons for such action at the only time when it might have been effective. Nearer the truth is surely Churchill's view that whatever Grey had done Germany was too deeply committed to withdraw.

Grey was not an able man in the sense of being intellectually brilliant, nor was he clever in the generally accepted meaning of that word. Where he excelled was in wisdom and judgement, both of which qualities were rooted in calm thought and breadth of outlook, while those who worked with him most closely have without exception paid tribute to his clear thinking and ability to go to the heart of any problem upon which he was called to pronounce. Asquith's Cabinet was one of the most outstanding in British history, and Grey was among its most outstanding members.

So far as the British people were concerned the crisis at the end of July and the beginning of August 1914 was very different from that a quarter of a century later. A European war in which Great Britain would be involved seemed such a remote possibility that little attention was paid to the prospect, so that when hostilities broke out it was as if a thunder-bolt had fallen. A small group in London, of which Leo Maxse was the most distinguished figure, had foreseen what was coming, but the mass of the population – of all classes – especially in the provinces, steadfastly refused to believe in the imminence of war. Interest in, and knowledge of, foreign affairs was confined to a few specialists in those days, and if the ordinary citizen thought about them at all it was in a very detached manner – almost as if they had been a sporting event. After all, there had been wars and crises in plenty during the previous ten years without

Britain becoming involved in them, and there seemed no special reason why the murder of an Archduke in an obscure Balkan town should prove an exception. This was the prevailing attitude even when July was already passing into August.

Nor were the issues at stake clear enough to stir the imagination. The Serbians were chiefly known for the brutal murder of their King and Queen not so long before, an atrocity which had caused Great Britain to suspend diplomatic relations with their country. When *John Bull* came out, only a few days before the war, with the poster 'To Hell with Servia' (as it was then usually spelt), its editor, Horatio Bottomley, was expressing the point of view of millions of his fellow countrymen. Britain's other prospective allies were not much more popular. Anti-Russian feeling had always been strong, and sympathy with Japan had been universal during the Russo-Japanese War. Tory dislike of Russia dated from the seventies, while Liberals and Socialists were not attracted by a régime which was opposed to everything in which they believed.

There was, it is true, considerable enthusiasm for France in certain circles in London, but elsewhere the old historic hostility had by no means died away, and the recent trial and acquittal of Madame Caillaux for the murder of Gaston Calmette, the editor of *Figaro*, whom she shot in his office, had done nothing to increase British respect for French institutions. On the other hand, there seemed no special reason to go to war with Austria-Hungary on behalf of the murderers of the heir to her throne and the nephew of her venerable monarch, for whom everyone had the highest admiration. Germany was admittedly another matter, and feeling had been hardening against her as the threat to British sea power became obvious; but in the early days of the crisis it was not very clear where she stood, and the quarrel seemed purely Balkan in its implications. As if this were not enough, there was every prospect of civil war in Ireland, so it was small wonder that attention was directed rather to Belfast than to Belgrade.

Then the Germans attacked Belgium, and at once the ranks were closed. The historical sense of the British people told them that this was an issue on which they would have to fight, and they did not hesitate. Why Germany committed the blunder of invading Belgium must always remain a good deal of a mystery, for events soon proved that this was no military necessity, for the French were not in a condition to resist or attack further east. Had Belgian neutrality been respected British intervention might have been delayed until it was too late, if it had taken place at all, for, as has been shown, opinion in the British Isles was generally very divided. As it was, the inevitable German gaffe was committed, and Great Britain came into the war.

81 The shape of things to come: 24 July 1909. Louis Blériot (1872–1936) at Calais shortly before his successful flight across the Channel in his Voisin machine.

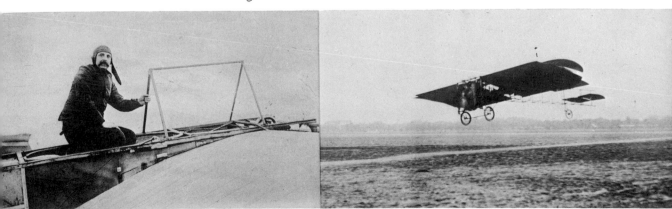

ACKNOWLEDGEMENTS

THE AUTHOR AND PUBLISHERS wish to record their grateful thanks to copyright owners for the use of the illustrations listed below:

To Barratt's Photo Press Ltd. for: 17
To William Gordon Davis for: 16
To Imperial War Museum for: 5
To the Mansell Collection for: 9, 10, 12 (and to *Illustrated London News*), 27, 28, 32, 40, 41, 45, 48, 50, 56, 62, 63 and 82 (and to *Punch*)
To Monitor Press Features Ltd. for: 46
To National Archives, Navy Department, Washington, D.C. for: 65
To National Library of Ireland for: 73 and 74
To George Outram & Co. Ltd. for: 75 and 76
To A. H. Poole, Waterford for: 26
To Paul Popper Ltd. for: 2, 4, 19, 20, 22, 30, 35, 38, 43, 49, 54, 55, 58, 59, 66, 67, 68, 69, 71, 72, 78 and 81
To *Radio Times* Hulton Picture Library for: title-page, 1, 3, 6, 7, 8, 11, 13, 14, 15, 18, 21, 23, 24, 25, 29, 31, 33, 34, 36, 37, 39, 42, 44, 47, 51, 52, 53, 57, 60, 64, 70, 77, 79 and 80
To United States Information Service for: 61

82   The World's Enemy
THE KAISER: '*Who goes there?*'
SPIRIT OF CARNAGE: '*A friend – your only one.*'
Punch, 19 August 1914

Index

Printed in Great Britain by Jarrold & Sons Limited, Norwich